JAPAN EMERGES

JAPAN EMERGES

A CONCISE HISTORY OF JAPAN
FROM ITS ORIGIN TO THE PRESENT

STEVEN WARSHAW AND C. DAVID BROMWELL
WITH A. J. TUDISCO

Distributed to Colleges and Universities by

CANFIELD PRESS

A Department of Harper & Row, Publishers, Inc.
San Francisco, California 94133

A Diablo Press/Canfield Press Publication

© 1964 and 1974 THE DIABLO PRESS
Berkeley and San Francisco
462 Coventry Road, Berkeley, California 94707

Printing History
First Edition as Part of ASIA EMERGES

First Printing
1964

Second Printing
1966

Third Printing
1967

Revised and Expanded as JAPAN EMERGES
1974

Second Printing as JAPAN EMERGES
1974

Library of Congress Catalog Card Number 73-93980

Library of Congress Cataloging in Publication Data

Warshaw, Steven.
    Japan emerges.

    (The Asia emerges series, 3)
    First published in 1964 as part of the Asia emerges, by
A. J. Tudisco; rev. and expanded.
    Bibliography. p.
    1. Japan—History. I. Bromwell, C. David, joint
author. II. Tudisco, A. J., joint author.
III. Tudisco, A. J., joint author.
III. Tudisco, A. J. Asia emerges. IV. Title.
DS835.W375   952   73-93980
ISBN 0-87297-016-7
ISBN 0-87297-017-5 (pbk.)

Printed in the United States of America

PREFACE

During the past thirty years, the Japanese have gained peacefully many of the objectives that could not be gained through war. Through concentrated effort, they have reconstructed their devastated nation and made it one of the most commercially successful and influential countries in the world. It is not likely that they have reached the limits of their success. Despite their lack of land and of raw materials, they have the courage, energy, and dedication that permits them to solve national problems with a speed that surprises less unified people.

Because not only Japan, but all of the rest of Asia has awakened from a long night, it has become urgent that its culture and context be studied in the West. In the recent past, historically speaking, the Japanese and other Asians were carefully analyzing the West. Their goal was to learn how new ideas and processes might help them to become modern powers. Using their own cultural foundations, they have now built economies and societies with which the West must deal and live. Indeed, most of the world's population, raw materials, and so perhaps its future, lies to the East.

The present book has its basis in *Asia Emerges*, a popular text which anticipated by almost a decade the need for concise materials about Asia. At that time Professor Chalmers Johnson, the noted specialist in Japan at the University of California, Berkeley, said of its Japanese section: "(This is) an excellent factual account of Japanese history from earliest times to the present. It covers all major aspects of Japanese political history, and I would recommend it highly."

Japan Emerges carefully brings the history of Japan up to the present time, emphasizing cultural and social as well as political and economic factors. It does not pretend to offer *original* scholarship in this complex field; certainly it is eclectic. It is presented in the hope that it will provide a bridge between English-speaking people and a civilization that is daily growing less remote.

ACKNOWLEDGMENTS

THIS BOOK HAS BEEN put to severe tests to insure its accuracy, completeness, and attractiveness to students and the public. Many people have helped. In its earlier form the material was used at length by hundreds of seniors in Berkeley High School, where it was sent in advance of publication. Their comments enabled us to refine the material, which then was presented to 200 other students, most of whom reported it immensely successful.

The material also was presented to readers who reviewed it with the precision that is characteristic of the best scholars in the field. They, and the positions that they held at the time of the reading, included Dr. Robert A. Scalapino, Professor and Chairman of the Department of Political Science, University of California, Berkeley, who is also frequently an adviser to the U.S. Department of State; Dr. Chalmers A. Johnson, who is identified above; and A. Elgin Heinz, Asia specialist and teacher of history, San Francisco Unified School District. They read the material up to Chapter 8. This material, here completely updated and revised, was reread, with ensuing parts, by Professor Delmer Brown of the University of California and Nancy Dyer, Research Assistant, Department of Asian Studies, University of California.

The illustrations for *Japan Emerges* were obtained from many sources. In particular, we wish to thank the following for their contributions: Frank Huggins, Associate Editor, *The Asian Student,* a publication of the Asia Foundation, San Francisco; Dr. Raymond N. Tang, Dr. Richard G. Irwin, Dr. Elizabeth Huff, and Chang-Soo Swanson, all of whom are or have been associated with the East Asiatic Library, University of California, Berkeley. A particular debt of gratitude is due to Arthur Miyazaki of that library, who helped to identify recently added pictures. We are also indebted to Rand McNally & Company and to the U.S. Government Printing Office, publisher of the Area Handbook Series, for providing maps or the basis of them. Finally, we are grateful to Fred Howell Jr., Berkeley attorney, for the legal efforts which enabled work on this book, and others in the Asia Emerges Series, to begin.

THE AUTHORS

CONTENTS

Preface, v
Acknowledgments, vi
Maps, ii, xi, xii, xiii

1

JAPAN IN PERSPECTIVE, 1–12
Land, 2–3
Rivers, 4
Climate, 4–5
Agriculture, 5–7
Forests, 7
Fishing, 7–9
Industry, 9–12

2

ANCIENT JAPAN:
EARLY HISTORY AND THE NARA PERIOD, 13–26
Early History, 13–15
Mythological origins. Early political and social organization.
Ancient Japanese Religion: Shinto, 16–17
Social Effects of Shinto, Shinto cult and priesthood.
The Influence of China, 17–19
The Great Taika Reforms. The Taiho Codes.
The Nara Period (710–784 A.D.), 19–26
Literary activity. Confucianism. Buddhism. Nara art.

3

THE HEIAN ERA AND THE KAMAKURA
SHOGUNATE, 27–38
Politics in the Heian Period (794–1185 A.D.), 27–29
Economic developments. The Taira-Minamoto conflicts.
Buddhism in the Heian Period, 29–30
The Tendai sect. The Shingon sect.
Heian Culture, 30–31
Literature. Heian art.

The Kamakura Shogunate (1186–1333 A.D.), 31–32
The Emergence of Japanese Feudalism, 32–34
The Evolution of Japanese Buddhism, 35–36
Amida Buddhism: the Jodo sect of Honen Shonin. The Lotus sect.
Zen Buddhism.
Kamakura Culture, 36–37
Painting.
Political Developments in the Kamakura Period, 37–38
Hojo Regency (1205–1333 A.D.). The Mongol invasions (1274–1281 A.D.).

4

**THE ASHIKAGA SHOGUNATE AND THE SENGOKU
PERIOD, 39–50**

The Ashikaga Shogunate (1338–1573 A.D.), 39–40
Ashikaga Culture: The Muromachi Period (1392–1573 A.D.), 40–42
The No drama. The tea ceremony. Art and architecture.
Religion under the Ashikaga, 42–43
Economic Developments under the Ashikaga, 43
A Time of Warfare: The Sengoku Period (1485–1568 A.D.), 44–48
*Political developments in the Sengoku. Hideyoshi's Korean
expeditions. The triumph of Tokugawa Ieyasu.*
Religious Developments: The Christian Missionaries, 48–50

5

**THE TOKUGAWA SHOGUNATE:
THE EDO PERIOD (1603–1867 A.D.), 51–64**

The Exclusion of Christian Missionaries and Merchants, 51–53
Tokugawa Society: The Final Stage of Feudalism, 53–56
Administration and law.
The Roots of Change in Tokugawa Japan, 56–57
Economic life.
Tokugawa Culture, 57–61
*Painting: the Ukiyo-e school. Tokugawa literature.
The popular stage: kabuki.*
The Decline of the Tokugawa Shogunate, 61–62
External Pressure: The End of Isolation, 62–64

6

MODERN JAPAN:
THE MEIJI RESTORATION (1868-1912), 65-81

The Meiji Reforms, 65-75
Social reform: the abolition of feudalism. Military and industrial
expansion. The Meiji Constitution. Education, religion, and law.
Meiji literature.

Japan as a World Power:
Foreign Expansion (1894-1918), 76-81
Sino-Japanese War (1894-1895). Russo-Japanese War (1904-1905).
Seizure of Korea (1910). World War I and the Twenty-One Demands.
Japan at the Versailles Peace Conference.

7

JAPAN BETWEEN THE TWO WORLD WARS, 82-92

Successes and Failure of Parliamentary Government
(1918-1931), 83-86
The Washington Conference (1921-1922).
Conflict between Parliament and the military (1924-1931).

The Triumph of the Military (1931-1937), 86-90
The Manchurian Incident (1931). Invasion of China (1937).
The Road to Total War, 90-92.

8

WAR, DEFEAT, AND REHABILITATION, 93-102

Allied Policies on Japan: Unconditional Surrender, 95-97
The American Occupation (1945-1951), 97-102
The new constitution. Economic and social reforms.

9

THE ENDURING JAPANESE CULTURE:
SOURCE OF NATIONAL PURPOSE, 103-114

The Family, 103-109
The hierarchical nature of the family. The extension of hierarchy.

The Legacy of History, 109–111
The Confucian basis of authority. The Tokugawa-Meiji heritage.
Japan in Transition, 111–114

10

INDEPENDENT JAPAN, 115–134
The cities. The country. Political groups. Government policies.
Present Policies, 127–134
The future of Japanese democracy.

Appendices

A. MOST POPULOUS NATIONS, 135

B. GUIDE TO THE PRONUNCIATION
OF JAPANESE WORDS, 135

C. GLOSSARY, 135–137

D. A CHRONOLOGY OF ASIAN HISTORY, 138–146

E. THE CONSTITUTION OF THE EMPIRE OF JAPAN, 147–156

F. THE IMPERIAL RESCRIPT RENOUNCING DIVINITY, 156–157

G. STATEMENT BY GENERAL DOUGLAS MACARTHUR, 158

H. THE CONSTITUTION OF JAPAN, 158–175

I. BIBLIOGRAPHY, 178

J. INDEX, 179–183

CITIES OF EASTERN AND SOUTHERN ASIA

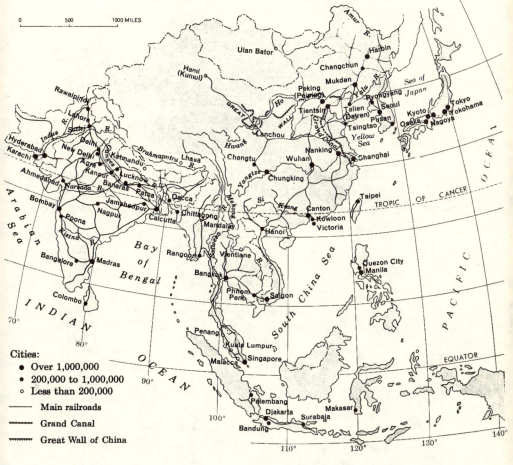

0   500   1000 MILES

Cities:
- ● Over 1,000,000
- ● 200,000 to 1,000,000
- ○ Less than 200,000

——— Main railroads

═══ Grand Canal

▬▬▬ Great Wall of China

© by Rand McNally & Co., R.L. 64-SF-11

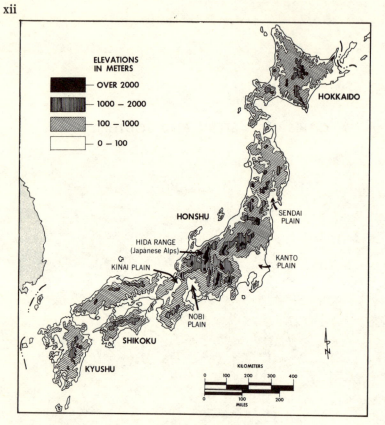

Elevations of Japan

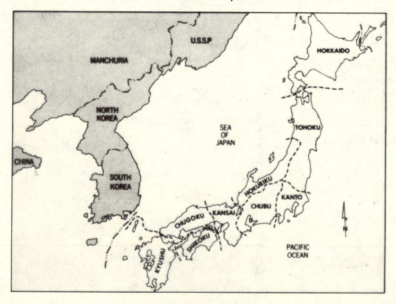

Natural Regions of Japan

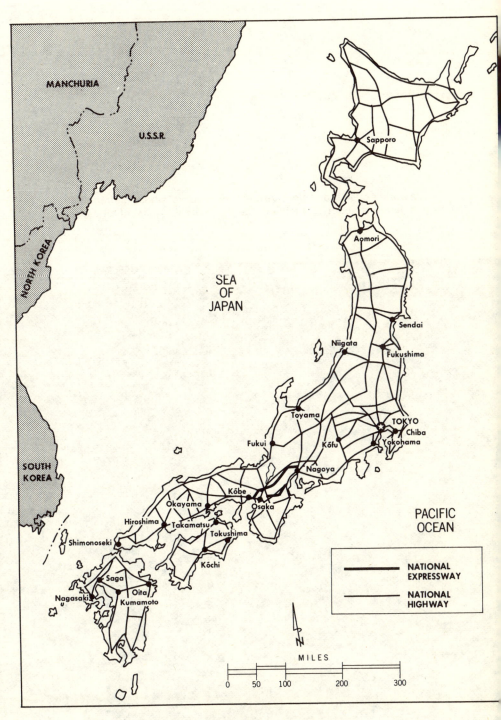

Cities and Highways of Japan

The world's busiest and most crowded city is Tokyo, whose metropolitan population is about 11.4 million. Its prosperity is typical of all Japan.

"Land of the Rising Sun"

CHAPTER 1

JAPAN IN PERSPECTIVE

JAPAN IS A CHAIN OF FOUR LARGE ISLANDS and many lesser islands lying off the mainland of Asia. Altogether, the Japanese islands cover 143,000 square miles, slightly less than the state of California. About four-fifths of the terrain is mountainous. A rocky mountain spine, running the length of the islands, is cross-cut by deep valleys and bordered by narrow coastal plains where most of the people live.

Far more than India and China, Japan is geographically isolated. This has helped it to develop a culture distinctly its own. Surrounded by the broad Sea of Japan on the west, the Sea of Okhotsk on the north, and the East China Sea to the south, the islands for centuries had little contact with continental Asia. The great intellectual and religious movements of India and China did not reach Japan until long after they began. In more recent times, the vast Pacific Ocean was a barrier to contact with America and Europe. During one long period (1640-1854) the Japanese government deliberately isolated the nation from Western influence.

Nevertheless, the Japanese have always been curious about the rest of the world and for more than 1,500 years have been borrowing ideas from the other countries. Concepts and institutions imported from China during the T'ang Dynasty (618-907 A.D.) profoundly influenced Japanese culture for the next thousand years. Around the middle of the nineteenth century Western science and technology burst upon the islands. Then the Japanese turned eagerly to the tasks of industrialization. In the past century, phenomenal scientific and industrial advances have greatly modified Japan's traditional institutions. Over its long history, the nation has preserved one language, one culture, and one dynasty. It has suffered only one successful invasion, in 1945. Now it has become more Western than Asian in many ways. Yet the Japanese have been reluctant to abandon many of their ancient customs and social patterns.

Today, Japan starkly contrasts modern and ancient ways of life—

1

electronics factories and hand-operated potter's wheels, television stations and medieval playhouses. Tokyo skyscrapers and wooden houses. Japan has gained the highest standard of living in Asia by fostering industrial growth. This progress, however, has not been without its price. It has greatly aggravated a long-standing problem —the pressure of population upon resources.

In 1867, the population of Japan was about 30,000,000. During the past century, largely because of industrialization and improved medical and sanitation facilities, it soared to its present level of 107,000,000. It is increasing at the rate of about 1,000,000 per year. The problem of providing food for these added millions is severe because there is so little land. Only a little more than 18 percent of the total acreage is arable. The largest region is the Kanto Plain outside Tokyo (5,000 square miles), where there are more than 14,000 people per square mile. Other concentrations are at Nagoya (the Nobi Plain) and Osaka (the Kansai Plain). There are at present more than 4,500 people for every square mile of cultivated land, the highest ratio of any country. By contrast, California with about 20 percent of the population of Japan, has 250 percent more arable land.

For over 1,500 years Japanese farmers have intensively cultivated their small plots of land. They achieve amazingly high yields considering the long periods the land has been worked. The Japanese diet is supplemented by large amounts of fish, shellfish, and other seafood. Nevertheless, every year the nation must import more than 15 percent of its basic food requirements.

To stem the population tide, Japan has in recent years introduced birth control. It is estimated that without birth control the annual increase would be near 2,000,000. Birth control, however, would not solve the entire problem. Like India and China, Japan is overpopulated, but, unlike them, cannot increase its farms. The country is now close to maximum crop production, especially in rice. Each year Japan becomes more dependent upon food imports, for which it pays by its exports of goods and services. The island nation must thus export to survive—a necessity that has become an explosive issue in Japanese politics. At present, Japan's population growth is no greater than that of any other industrialized country. Yet its central problem remains the relationship between its population and its land, only 20 percent of which is usable.

LAND

The islands of the Japanese archipelago are strung out between 30 and 45 degrees north latitude. From south to north, the four main islands are Kyushu, Shikoku, Honshu, and Hokkaido. Honshu which literally means "main island," is the largest. Shikoku is the smallest.

Before the ancestors of the Japanese came to settle on Kyushu and then moved north to the other islands, a people called the Ainu occupied the land. Northern Hokkaido is the last refuge of this Caucasian people. The Ainu were steadily driven from the islands to the south. The Japanese considered them barbarians and took their lands much as the white man took the lands of the Indians in the United States. Only during the past century have many Japanese moved as far north as Hokkaido.

The Japanese islands are dominated by a series of rugged mountain chains, topped by majestic volcanic cones. In the Japanese Alps, or Hida Range, on central Honshu, peaks soar to above 10,000 feet. Mount Fuji, or Fujiyama (12,388 feet), the most famous mountain of this range, last erupted in the eighteenth century. Mount Sakura (3,688 feet) in the harbor of Kagoshima, Kyushu, is still active. In addition to the volcanoes, the islands have many volcanic hot springs which are used for bathing.

Japan has nearly 17,000 miles of coastline. The best harbors are on the Pacific and along the shores of the Inland Sea, which lies between Honshu, Shikoku, and Kyushu. The islands are very narrow and, from an airplane flying about 18,000 feet, one can see the Pacific Ocean on the east and the Sea of Japan on the west.

Most villages in the center of Honshu island have views of Mount Fuji (12,388 feet). Once considered the home of spirits, it last erupted in 1707.

RIVERS

Japanese rivers are short, swift, and shallow, and few of them are navigable. They rise in the mountains and, because of their rapid drop in elevation, flow swiftly to the sea. The most important river is the Tone, which drains through the eastern Kanto Plain. Japan's swift-flowing streams can cause serious erosion. For centuries the islanders have taken great pains to control them. Proof of their efforts are the dykes and stone embankments which dot the countryside.

The rivers are harnessed for hydroelectric power and used for irrigation. Irrigation systems, however, are not as elaborate as those in India or China. With abundant rainfall, the need for extensive irrigation does not arise.

CLIMATE

Japan has a widely varying climate. The island chain, if super-imposed on the United States, would stretch roughly from Maine to Florida. The differences in climate would be about the same as between these two states. Subtropical Kyushu has temperatures similar to those in Georgia, while wintry Hokkaido has a climate like that of Maine. In general, the surrounding waters have a moderating influence on temperatures.

Japan's climate is directly affected by two ocean currents, one warm and the other cold. The warm current, the *Kuroshio*, or Japan Current, flows from the tropical regions near the Philippine Islands. It runs along the east coast of Japan to the area of Tokyo, then swings northeast into the Pacific. The cold current, the *Oyashio*, moves southward from the Sea of Okhotsk. It also follows the eastern coast of Japan until it mingles with the warm Japan Current between Tokyo and Sendai. Western Japan is chilled by bitter Arctic winds that blow over the Sea of Japan during the winter.

Rainfall in Japan is determined largely by the winter and summer monsoons. From October to March dry cold polar air moves east from the interior of Siberia toward the Pacific. Crossing the Sea of Japan, the winter monsoon absorbs moisture and drops it on the western side of the islands. This region is covered with heavy snow. In some villages the snowfall is so heavy that the inhabitants must tunnel beneath the drifts to get from one building to another. But because the mountains block the winter winds, the eastern side of the islands receive much less snow.

From late April through September, temperatures in continental Asia are mild. The summer monsoon blows up from the southeast over the Pacific, bringing warm rains. June and July are the Japanese rainy season. Most of the islands receive between 40 and 120 inches of rainfall. The heavy precipitation and high temperatures make rice cultivation possible. This is considered the time to plant seedlings. In

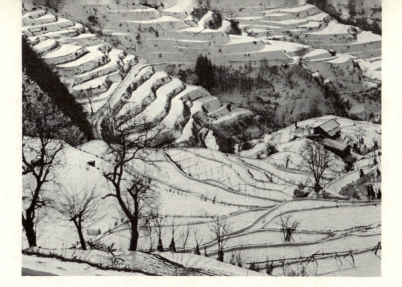

Winter snows cover the steep hillsides of northern Japan. The slopes have been terraced so that more of the land can be used for agriculture.

the three southern islands, sporadic rains and uncomfortably hot temperatures last until September. Hokkaido enjoys moderate summer temperatures because of the cooling *Oyashio* current. May to October is also the typhoon season. These violent storms form in the Caroline, Marshall, and Mariana Islands, sweeping up from the south about twice a month.

April and October are the most pleasant months of the Japanese year. In April, city parks and the countryside come to life with blossoming cherry trees, a delight to both the nature-loving Japanese and foreign visitors. In picturesque October, the land is ablaze with turning maple leaves and the golden hue of ripened rice. Throughout the summer Japan's forests are lush, cool, and inviting; and the famous Japanese gardens, with their rocks, artificial waterfalls, dwarf trees, and flowering shrubs, are a joy to behold.

AGRICULTURE

Japan's abundant summer rainfall and warm climate make possible a long growing season. In fields and paddies from Kyushu to about 100 miles north of Tokyo, it is possible to grow two crops a year. If it were not for this two-crop system, Japan would be forced to import at least half of its foodstuffs.

The first crop is usually wheat or barley, which is planted in late fall and harvested by mid-June. The second crop is rice, usually planted in late June and harvested during September. In October, between the rice and wheat seasons, many farmers grow vegetables between the rows of wheat and barley. This crop matures rapidly and does not interfere with the slower-growing grains.

The Japanese farmland is either irrigated paddy land or upland fields that are watered naturally. Farmers struggle to farm their mountainous terrain. Paddy land must be nearly level so that it can be flooded during the time the rice is growing. A slope is required, however, so that the paddy can be drained and the rice permitted to ripen. This drainage is also necessary to prevent flooding during the winter months when the paddy land is being used for wheat or barley.

Japan's large harvests are partly the result of soil conservation. For centuries, Japanese farmers have practiced composting, fertilization, and erosion control. The soils have thus remained fertile despite a thousand years of use. Without these techniques, they would have been depleted long ago.

The Japanese also have extensive fruit-growing and dairying industries. The country is famous for its persimmons, tangerines, and melons. Because of the strong influence of Buddhism, which prohibits meat eating and milk drinking, dairying did not develop until late in the nineteenth century. Since World War I, however, many more Japanese have begun to eat meat and to drink milk. Hokkaido is the center of Japan's dairy industry. On the island, modern dairy

Many Japanese farmers still thresh grain with primitive hand flails. Wheat and barley are planted in the late fall and are harvested in late spring.

farms, resembling those in the United States and Denmark, produce milk, butter, and cheese in large quantities.

FORESTS

Japan is one of the world's most heavily forested countries, an amazing fact considering the large population concentrated in the relatively small area of the islands. About 60 percent of the area is forests. More than half of these forests are of broadleaf trees.

Lumbering and pulp-making are the major forest industries. Japan's wood is also used in the manufacture of synthetic fibers and plastics. Another important product of the forests is charcoal, which is used for cooking and heating purposes. Until recently, most Japanese houses did not have central oil or gas heating. In winter, heat was supplied mainly by small charcoal braziers. Winter in Hokkaido, where the cold is severe, became known as the "season of stoves." But the Japanese have been using less charcoal for heating as their prosperity has increased. Central heating has become common.

For over three hundred years, the Japanese government has prevented excessive cutting of trees. Since 1875, it has enforced reforestation. The amount of timber which may be cut is determined by the amount of new growth each year. To conserve their forests, the Japanese import much of their timber. Scientific forest management is widespread, and privately owned lands are as carefully managed as the state-controlled forests. Yet much wood is imported.

FISHING

Japan is a great fishing nation. Fish and fish products are the main source of protein in the Japanese diet, and second only to rice in importance.

Eighty percent of Japanese fishing is coastal, most of it done within a range of five miles from shore. Coastal fishing is usually practiced on a modest scale. The fishermen are most often farmers who supplement their income by fishing at certain times of the year. Small farming-fishing villages are found all along the coasts. In these villages fishing is usually a family activity, with one boat operated by the entire household. Some villages conduct fishing as a community venture in which all households share in the work and the profits. As a household activity, the fishing is sometimes done by the men, while farming is left to the women.

The villages which are forced to depend entirely upon the sea for a livelihood are the most poverty-stricken in Japan. In villages where farming is the main activity and fishing only secondary, the people are generally more prosperous. Although often poor, Japanese villagers are friendly and hospitable. Poverty has created a marked equality between men and women in these villages.

On the Shima Peninsula, these women are among the several thousand who dive for cultured pearls and supply a great industry.

The remaining 20 percent of Japanese fishing is in the far seas, where Japanese commercial fleets conduct a large and profitable business. By adapting modern techniques to their industry, Japanese fishermen have consistently increased their annual "catch." They have used sonar to find large schools of fish. Since the 1930's they have been sending "floating factories" onto the high seas to accompany motor-driven fishing craft. These large vessels store and refrigerate fish for the small ones, which thus can work more effectively. Fishermen mostly catch tuna, salmon, and halibut.

The operations of Japanese trawlers in the Pacific have led to disputes with the United States, Canada, Russia, China, and Korea. The Americans and Canadians have limited Japanese fishing around Alaska and British Columbia, while the Russians have done the same along the coast of Siberia and the Kamchatka Peninsula. Communist China has warned Japanese fishermen to respect its territorial waters. Korea has seized Japanese vessels sighted off its shores. These restrictions are a great concern to Japan because of its great need for fish—both to consume and to export.

A unique aspect of Japan's use of the sea has been its development of the cultured-pearl industry. A Japanese named Mikimoto learned how to implant in the oyster a small seed around which a pearl forms. After the seeds have been inserted, the oysters are put in wire cages in the sea for one to ten years. The longer the seed remains in the oyster, the more valuable the pearl. Except by use of X rays, it is impossible to distinguish a fine cultured pearl from a natural one. A sizable Japanese cultured pearl industry has grown up. Its products, sold to many countries, are an important source of foreign exchange.

In addition to fish, the Japanese harvest large amounts of seaweed from the surrounding oceans. Various types of edible seaweed enrich the nation's diet. Some seaweeds are also used to make medicines such as iodine. These have become important to Japanese trade.

INDUSTRY

Japanese industry was begun to prevent Western military and economic penetration. When, in 1867, the nation emerged from long isolation, Japan's rulers wanted to avoid China's forced economic and territorial concessions to Western powers. Consequently, the first industries were military ones.

From the outset, Japan's industry has been handicapped by a lack of mineral wealth. The islands have many minerals but only coal is found in large amounts. During World War II, Japanese militarists planned to solve this problem by taking over Southeast Asia. There it hoped to gain rich deposits of coal, petroleum, bauxite, manganese, and other resources. Having failed in conquest, since 1945 Japan has turned to importing minerals.

Coal, although abundant in Kyushu and Hokkaido, is of poor quality. The country lacks the anthracite and coking coal essential to the iron and steel industry. The problem of coking coal has been especially acute since the end of World War II. Before the war, Japan obtained this fuel from Manchuria after seizing that land from China in 1931. With the loss of Manchuria, the Japanese have been forced to import coking coal, principally from the United States. The increased cost has handicapped Japan in the international iron and steel markets.

Japan is also short of petroleum, the second great source of industrial power. Some small petroleum deposits exist at Niigata and Akita, as well as along the western coast of Hokkaido. But these deposits do not begin to meet the needs of industry. Japan has been forced to import about 95 percent of its petroleum requirements from the Middle East, Indonesia, and the United States. Because of a shortage of dollars, Japan has, in recent years, been trying to shift its imports from the United States' fields to those of the Middle East. In the winter of 1973–74, this policy caused Japan grave difficulties. At a point when almost 88 percent of its oil was being imported from the Middle East, the governments controlling the supply announced sharp increases in price. The same Middle East governments were restricting oil shipments to the United States and Europe in an effort to apply indirect political pressure on Israel. As a result, Japan had no alternative but to pay the higher price and thus to reduce its rate of growth. Nevertheless, it moved speedily to insure delivery of Middle East oil. First, it agreed to support the oil-producing countries diplomatically. Second, it arranged to make investments in the Middle

East, particularly Iran. There, it helped to finance construction of a $2 billion oil refinery and a $900 million petro-chemical plant. Most of the products of both of these huge developments were scheduled to go to Japan.

As noted earlier, Japan has developed its hydroelectric power, the third great source of industrial energy, to the maximum. The shortness of rivers and the lack of storage reservoirs make it impossible to build giant hydroelectric plants so common in the United States. Nevertheless, electricity is used extensively in Japan, both industrially and commercially.

In spite of the lack of necessary minerals, Japan has become the leading industrial power in Asia. Material deficiences have been largely compensated for by one great natural source which the nation has in abundance—manpower. Japan early developed a system of public education which provided the country with trained technicians. Today, Japan has the best-trained industrial force in Asia. Thus, overpopulation, Japan's curse, is also of benefit.

In its early stages, Japanese industry was government financed. There were no capitalists in Japan with resources to build and operate large enterprises. Most investments came from a heavy tax upon the peasants, who thus were burdened with converting the country into an industrial nation. After the industries were built and operating, the government sold them at low cost to a few private investors. The result was the rise of a few financial families, known as the *zaibatsu* (literally, "money clique"), who rapidly gained control of the entire Japanese economy.

The four most powerful families of the zaibatsu were Mitsui, Mitsubishi, Yasuda, and Sumitomo. In pre-World War II Japan, these families controlled 70 percent of all bank deposits. Three of them controlled more than 50 percent of the coal output and over 50 percent of the merchant shipping. Mitsui and Mitsubishi were dominating powers in two political parties. They were able to manipulate governmental fiscal policies in order to gain huge subsidies. In addition, their control of banks, trust companies, and insurance firms enabled them to influence the rest of the economy. Although after World War II the American occupation authorities tried to break up the zaibatsu, the money clique has since been reviving. Since World War II the success of Japan's economy has enabled its financial institutions to prosper as never before. Six of the twenty largest banks in the world are Japanese. For the most part, they are dominated by the heirs of the zaibatsu. Thus the Sumitomo and Mitsubishi families remain powerful in Japan. Unlike the United States, Japan does not seek to prevent its banks from investing in other industries. Its banks, therefore, have growing power and are investing throughout the world.

The last head of the Mitsubishi zaibatsu was Koyata Iwasaki, shown here with his wife. After World War II the zaibatsu were ordered dissolved.

Japanese industry is concentrated in a few areas. Tokyo-Yokohama is the largest manufacturing area, followed by the Osaka-Kobe region. The largest iron-and-steel complex, the Yawata firm, is situated in northern Kyushu. Japan's shipbuilding industry, which centers on the port of Yokohama, is the world's largest. Before World War II, Japan owned one of the world's biggest merchant fleets. Most of it was sunk by American submarines during the war. In the past decade, however, Japan has been building its fleet at a rapid rate. Besides building ships for its own domestic firms, the Japanese shipbuilding industry now constructs oil tankers, freighters, and other vessels for many foreign countries, including the United States.

Japan has scores of other industries. The most important include electrical machinery, electronics, textiles, tool and die, automobiles, bicycles, watches, and toys. The Japanese optical goods industry is one of the finest in the world. Japanese cameras such as the Nikon and

The Japanese electronics industry is booming. These women are assembling television sets, many of which will be exported throughout the world.

Canon are superb precision instruments. All Japanese industries benefit from government-run communications systems. Railroads link all parts of the nation, and trains in Japan are rarely late. The government also operates efficient telephone and telegraph systems.

Apart from the huge zaibatsu combine, most Japanese firms are small, usually employing fewer than one hundred workers. A prime characteristic of all Japanese industry is paternalism. Employers take a direct, personal interest in caring for the welfare of their employees. Business practices which, to the casual Western observer, often seem inefficient make sense given the nation's special problems such as overpopulation. For example, by hiring many employees for short hours instead of a few for a full day's work, Japanese employers make jobs available for millions more workers. Working and living conditions of Japanese workers are still below United States standards. But Japan, at least, has avoided the unemployment which faces many Western industrial countries.

CHAPTER 2

ANCIENT JAPAN: EARLY HISTORY AND THE NARA PERIOD

THE JAPANESE ISLANDS lie in an arc close to the continent of Asia. Because of this proximity, it appears that the people who first lived in Japan came from both northern and southern Asia and crossed from the mainland to the nearest points on the islands. In the north, Mongols and Tungus came from Korea, as well as a unique group of Caucasians, the Ainu. From southern China others, including Malayans, migrated to Japan. The mingling of these stocks produced the Japanese people.

Archeology traces Japanese culture back to the Neolithic period. Two distinct types of pottery of that period, about 6,000 years old, are the ancient *jomon* ("rope pattern") pottery, characterized by rope-like designs; and the more advanced *Yayoi* pottery, named after the town where it was found. Similarities between Yayoi pottery (as well as numerous *magatama*, or "curved jewels" made from stone, bone, and horn) and other artifacts discovered in Korea and Manchuria support the theories of early migrations from northern Asia.

The theory that the Japanese are also related to the peoples of southern Asia is based on psychological impressions rather than archeological finds. Some peculiarities of custom, speech, diet, and dwelling of the inhabitants of southern Japan show similarities to such Southeast Asian peoples as the Indochinese and Malayans. Rice culture is assumed to have come to Japan from southern China. The construction of houses on poles over water, characteristic of the southern island of Kyushu, resembles the technique of the peoples of Malaya.

EARLY HISTORY

Writing was late to develop in Japan, compared with India and China. Because of this, the origins of the Japanese people are obscure. The Japanese themselves account for their beginnings in elaborate myths and legends. These stories have helped to formulate the basic attitudes of the Japanese. They have been supported by the leaders of the nation and are strongly believed by millions of people.

Mythological origins. Japan is said to have been created by the deities Izangi and Izanami, representatives of the male and female principles. This pair gave birth to many deities, including Amate-

13

Resembling a rope, the pattern
on this pot was typical
during Japan's Jomon, or
Rope Pattern Period.

rasu-O-mi-kami, the sun goddess, and Susa-no-wo, the storm god, who fought for authority over succeeding gods. Amaterasu, who represents light, triumphed over her brother, Susa-no-wo.

Later Amaterasu-O-mi-kami sent messengers to Izumo, where the descendants of her brother were installed. A compromise was reached whereby the descendants of the sun goddess would have dominion over secular Japan, while Susa-no-wo's offspring would control religious activities. After the agreement was reached, the grandson of Amaterasu arrived on the island of Kyushu. Jimmu Tenno, the first emperor of Japan, is said to be the direct descendant of Amaterasu's grandson, whom she assigned to rule Japan. Traditionally, the Japanese claim their history begins with the arrival of Amaterasu's grandson in 600 B.C. Scholars believe that Japan's origin was much later, with the migration of mainland people to the island. But the Japanese prefer generally to believe the myth.

Early political and social organization. It is only in the late fifth century A.D. with the appearance of chronicles written in Chinese that our knowledge of early Japan becomes fairly accurate. A Japanese written language did not appear until much later. On the basis of the early chronicles and brief mention of Japan in Chinese and Korean histories, a general picture may be drawn.

The most important cultural center during that century was on the Yamato Peninsula in southern Honshu, south of today's cities of Nara and Kyoto. It is believed that the Yamato clan, headed by the emperor Jimmu-Tenno, migrated from Kyushu to this region where it established its authority over all rival powers. "Japan," at that time, was limited to northern Kyushu and southern Honshu. The northern part of Honshu was occupied by the "barbarian" Ainu. The land was known as *Nippon, Nikon,* or *Nihon* (roughly "Land of the Rising Sun.").

In the early centuries of the Christian era, Japanese society was highly decentralized. Throughout the islands power was split among a number of warring clans. Each clan was governed by a chieftain, who was its religious and political leader. A clan worshipped its own deity, followed its own customs and beliefs, and possessed its own lands. Every clan member considered himself a descendant of the common deity.

The clan was broken down into a rigid hierarchy, with the chieftain and his family forming the aristocratic class. At the lower levels were lesser lords, free peasants, and others whose exact status depended upon heredity and occupation. The Yamato clan was headed by the emperor, who, through Jimmu-Tenno, claimed direct descent from Amaterasu-O-mi-kami, the sun goddess. The emperor ruled all Japanese who worshipped the sun goddess. In theory, the emperor had power over all clan chieftains, but in reality he controlled only his own clan. His title, Tenno, means "Born of Heaven."

In this period, Japanese life was predominantly agricultural, with rice as the basic crop. There was also hunting and fishing. Since the farmers looked upon the sun as the source of good harvests, it was natural that the Japanese paid highest homage to the sun goddess. Because of their strong ties to the land, the Japanese also worshipped other deities of nature.

The Ainu, who have white skin and beards, lived in Japan in prehistoric times. They were driven to the island of Hokkaido, where many still live.

ANCIENT JAPANESE RELIGION: SHINTO

The indigenous religion of Japan is *Shinto*, which means "Way of the gods." Originally, it had few doctrines and was considered nothing more than a cult which embodied the traditions and sentiments of the Japanese people. Shinto emphasized the importance of the family and communal life, the virtues of valor and fidelity, and the idea of national unity. Above all, the Shinto creed of the divine origin of the emperor helped to preserve Japanese society through centuries of discord.

In Shinto doctrine, the spirits, or deities, are called *kami*, which means "superior," "sacred," or "miraculous." Any object which evoked a sense of mystery was regarded as a kami and accorded due respect. These kami were thought to reside everywhere in nature. Thus, in a sense, Shinto was a form of nature worship. It had no complex basis, such as Buddhism's promise of life after death.

Social effects of Shinto. In traditional Japan, Shinto became intimately bound up with the life of the clan. Each clan claimed descent from a particular deity, or kami. The cult of this kami was the center of all communal life, influencing the beliefs and customs of the people. The clan kami was usually represented by a symbol that was enshrined in a simple sanctuary. The shrine was always situated in the woods for the divine spirits to live in.

Shinto demanded absolute fidelity to the clan and its traditions. This ideal vastly strengthened group solidarity but prevented self-expression. In fact, the individual ordinarily amounted to little in the community. But though Shinto morality stressed submission to authority, it also encouraged aggressive militarism. In later history, loyalty to the clan was transferred to the centralized state under the emperor.

Another general effect of Shinto was to promote purity and cleanliness in daily life. In Shinto belief, a great offense was that of polluting oneself by any contact with death, disease, blood, or the process of childbirth. Such pollution required cleansing by bathing in a stream, followed by a period of fasting. The popularity of bathing in modern Japan can be traced to the influence of Shinto.

Shinto cult and priesthood. Throughout Japanese history, the Shinto sanctuary has remained a simple structure, exemplifying the virtues of purity and austerity. The sanctuary is enclosed by fences and trees, planted around a square, and is marked by a sanctified rope of straw. The shrine itself rests on plain pillars and is covered with a thatched roof. The best-known feature of all Shinto shrines is the portal, or *tori-i*. This gateway, made of either stone or wood, consists of two quadrangular beams laid horizontally atop round columns. The tori-i usually stands at the entrance to the sanctuary at

The largest tori-i in Japan is at Kyoto's Heian Shrine. The word tori-i means "where the bird perches."

the head of a long avenue of trees.

In small villages that cannot afford a shrine the Japanese erect a pole of weed or bamboo. Pieces of paper or cloth, called the *gohei* (paper strips symbolizing offerings of clothing) or the *nusa* (paper or cloth strips used as a wand for the act of purification), are inserted through the pole.

The Shinto ceremony is very simple and quiet. There is no image in the shrine, but only a symbol of the kami, usually a mirror. The offering to the kami consists of a specially arranged dish of food and a cup of sake. Human sacrifices were not allowed by Shinto because bloodshed was considered an impure act. Most Shinto ceremonies are conducted publicly by a priest in absolute silence. However, dances with musical accompaniment may be held in another building. The dance frequently portrays a scene from a myth.

The priesthood is hereditary in certain Japanese families who claim descent from the gods. Shinto priests are allowed to marry. They have therefore been able to bestow power on heirs and keep outsiders from becoming priests. In ancient Japan, for example, the priestly family of Nakatomi was a powerful force in Yamato until Buddhists displaced them.

The Influence of China

In 538 A.D. a Korean ruler sent a Buddhist teacher and several Buddhist works of art to the Japanese imperial court. To test the appeal of Buddhism among the feudal lords, the emperor required the Soga clan to adopt Buddhism for a trial period. Immediately the

Mononobe, a warrior clan, and the Nakatomi, the priestly clan, turned against the Sogas. Civil wars ensued among the clans. While the struggle continued, more Buddhist missions reached the islands from China. They brought the high arts of writing and painting, as well as medical and scientific skills. As we will see, these powerful attractions later made Buddhism more popular than Shintoism.

In 593 A.D. Crown Prince Shotoku, governing Japan for a young emperor, became impressed with Buddhism and declared it the favored religion. He sent monks and students to China to observe the institutions that had developed on the mainland. The students were astonished by the wealth, power, and efficient governments of the then-flourishing Sui and T'ang dynasties, which favored Buddhism. Before long, Buddhist and Confucian concepts, and Chinese ideas of politics and law, began to flow to Japan. Buddhist temples, schools, and hospitals were also built during Shotoku's thirty-year reign. He is said to be the author of the Constitution of Seventeen Articles (604 A.D.), which urged self-discipline and morality and so prepared the way for reform.

The Great Taika Reforms.   By 645 A.D. the Fujiwara clan had gained control of the imperial court. Under its influence the Taika Reforms (Taika means "great change") were introduced. These reforms, inspired by the Chinese example, directly attacked the Japanese clan system. They ended landholding by clans and brought the nation under the emperor's control. Henceforth, all land was his. Governors were appointed to administer the several regions of the country and taxation was established. To appease the clan chieftains, who were losing authority, the Fujiwara rulers granted them important government positions and high ranks in the court nobility.

Traditional festivals, like this modern one, were highly dramatic events in the lives of villagers. The Shinto cult stressed group solidarity.

These reforms were possible because the strongest clan chieftains supported the Fujiwaras. Yet, although the Taika Reforms brought about great changes, they did not affect the basic structure of society—the nobility and free peasants. The peasants, freed from the rule of the clan chieftains, were not subject to the state.

The Taiho Codes. The powerful influence of China was at its peak with the institution of the Taiho Codes in 702 A.D. These codes, a legal record of earlier Taika Reforms, shaped Japanese life for the next five hundred years. They converted the country from a loose federation of clans to a highly centralized nation. Under them, the emperor appointed officials from the ranks of the nobility and allotted peasants a fixed acreage to farm. He assigned governors to administer the provinces and collect taxes.

With the breakup of the power of clans, the family became the prime unit of social organization. Authority rested with the head of the family, the father. No member of the family could marry or choose an occupation without his approval. In the villages families were organized into small cooperative groups, called *kumi.* Each household of the kumi helped to establish the way of life in its group. Each community, in turn, was placed under the authority of a headman and a council.

The Taiho Codes also set up a system of public education, but only for the sons of the nobility. The curriculum reflected the strong influence of Chinese classics, literature, ethics, and law. As in China, the primary aim of education was to train civil servants. But while in China government jobs were theoretically available to anyone who passed the examinations, in Japan those posts, like education, were only open to the nobility. The effect of this policy was to sharpen the division between the rulers and the ruled. In Japan, the upper class was trained in Chinese ethics and values, while the common people were left to educate themselves until the thirteenth century.

The Taiho Codes, while bringing the benefits of Chinese political centralization, also introduced some of its liabilities. China's land policies gave the peasants fixed acreages but also enriched greedy officials. The same was true in Japan. Japanese officials were exempted from paying taxes; the burden thus fell on the free peasants. Moreover, lesser revenue officials, like their Chinese cousins, began to cheat the government.

THE NARA PERIOD (710–784 A.D.)

The success of the central government forced Japan's rulers to build a larger capital. At the site of the town of Nara a capital was built on the model of Ch'ang-an, capital of China's T'ang Dynasty. The construction of a permanent capital was a sign of the waning influence of Shinto and the rise of Buddhism, for Nara was a center of

The calligraphy at left, cast into a Nara temple bell, uses Chinese characters (*kanji*) to represent Japanese sounds. Part of the same calligraphy is shown at right, rendered in another form of kanji which is called *kana*.

Buddhist activity. The death of the emperor was the main reason for changing the place of the capital. Death was thought to pollute a site. A new emperor customarily moved to a new capital. The names of each site have therefore become a convenient reference to various periods of Japanese history. The names of rulers or ruling families may also be used.

Following the example of the Chinese T'ang government, the Nara rulers divided Japan into provinces, districts, townships, and communities. At the highest level, an imperial council was established with sweeping administrative powers. The council was aided by a board of ministers. Each provincial governor was granted authority to levy and collect taxes, conscript for public works projects and military service, and try court cases. These governors along with lesser officials on the district and township levels, were ranked in an elaborate hierarchy.

Literary activity. In the Nara period, Chinese influence was not limited to politics. The study of Chinese language and literature became the chief intellectual pastime of the court aristocracy. The University of Nara, which specialized in Chinese subjects, was open to the sons of nobles and officials of high rank. Unlike the Chinese, Japanese scholars were not interested in spreading knowledge to the common people. Learning was, rather, an ornament of the privileged class.

The study of Chinese literature forced the Japanese to learn the Chinese script. The Japanese had no written language of their own. They succeeded in applying Chinese characters phonetically to their own spoken language. Thus the word "Nara" could be written by using two Chinese characters whose reading approximated the sounds of "na" and "ra."

However, Chinese characters hampered literary expression and so forced more linguistic change. After some of them were made to represent Japanese words purely through their sounds, others were adopted to expand the number of meanings. A combination of the two syllabaries provided the Japanese more ways to express themselves in literature, especially in poetry. At length usage reduced certain phonetically employed characters to symbols. These symbols represented the forty-eight sounds of the Japanese language. They were called *kana*, literally "borrowed names," and were later developed into a cursial form called hiragana (literally, "smooth kana"). However, Chinese characters, called *kanji*, were and still are retained. They are much more numerous than the kana and so are more difficult to learn. Unlike Chinese, Japanese words change according to their position in a sentence. Modified versions of the ancient Chinese forms also are used to render foreign words into Japanese.

Japanese verbal language did not change as a result of the use of Chinese writing, although many new words were imported. As they gained a written language, the Japanese quickly began their great literary tradition through such works as *Kojiku* ("Records of Ancient Matters") and *Nihongi* ("Chronicles of Japan"). Dealing with the mythological history of Japan and the geneology of its rulers, they resemble contemporary Chinese interests. By the eighth century the Japanese were able to use their language more freely and began to develop the *Manyoshu*, a collection of some of the most beautiful songs and poems that had been written in Japan.

Confucianism. Their admiration for China's T'ang Dynasty caused the rulers of Japan to consider the sources of Chinese power. Confucianism appeared to be one of the principal links binding China's people to their government. It contained elements of a philosophy which the Chinese people had been developing since prehistoric times. However, it was assembled, codified, and taught by Confucius and his followers and so bore his name.

Born in 551 B.C., Confucius was raised in a period of incessant warfare and pledged himself to the cause of peace. The Five Classics, a series of books in which his followers embodied his philosophy, stated that peace could be obtained through *jen* (pronounced "ren," meaning humanitarianism"). In practice, jen could be achieved through a sense of propriety. If all persons knew how to deal with all others, there would be peace.

Confucianism suggested that there was a natural order in the universe. Man, as part of it, was obliged to respect this order, not to disturb it. In the family, the natural head was the father. His wife and children treated him with reverence and esteem. He, in turn, treated them benevolently. The reciprocal relationships between all family members and, indeed, all others, too, were known and respected.

In the field of government, one of the most important Confucian traditions was first proclaimed by Mencius (371–289 B.C.). He is regarded as the leading apostle of Confucius. He reasoned that since all men are responsible to a universal order, the emperor can be no exception. In the view of Mencius, the emperor was responsible to "Heaven," an abstract force not at all like the Christian God. While his rule was proper and benevolent, the emperor had the "Mandate of Heaven." That is, if he ruled correctly, Heaven would be pleased. However, Heaven could be displeased by incorrect rule. If it were, it would send a sign, such as a comet or eclipse. It would trouble his administration with droughts or floods. Once they recognized that he had lost the Mandate, the people had the duty to replace the emperor.

When transferred to Japan, many of these Chinese concepts were placed within the framework of government or society. There they were subtly changed, however, to fit the Japanese way of life. In the family, Confucianism was used to create relationships that were less reciprocal than pyramidal. We will see later how the hierarchy in family life was used to create not benevolence, but deference to authority. The Japanese did not acknowledge that their emperor could be deposed. Descended from the gods, a divinity on earth, he was undeniably the head of state. The Mandate of Heaven could not be withdrawn from him.

Nor did the Japanese accept the Chinese idea that any adult male could become a member of the government. In China, this was inferred by the fact that anyone could take the civil service examination leading to a government post, although in practice only the wealthy could study long enough to pass the difficult test. Any suggestion of reliance on talent did not appeal to the wealthy Japanese. They preferred a system in which noble birth and character, rather than ability to pass an examination, determined who would govern the country.

Despite these important exceptions, the Japanese faithfully imported the structure of Confucianism, if not its true philosophy. With it they brought the astrology and divination that were considered vital to the Chinese court. Through the Five Classics they carefully incorporated Chinese concepts in their institutions. A Japanese constitution of the Taiho Code period quotes the *Analects*, one of the Four Sacred Books of Confucianism: "Heaven shelters, Earth upbears." That is, the way of Heaven is permanent; those below must obey.

Buddhism. The great leader of Buddhism was Siddhartha Gautama, an Indian prince of the sixth century. Gautama experienced every earthly pleasure, but at the age of twenty-nine renounced this life in order to seek the causes of human suffering. He wandered for six years. At length, while meditating for forty-nine days beneath a tree near Benaras, India, he developed a concept that was to become one of the great philosophies of the world. Gautama's first speech, the "Sermon of the Turning of the Wheel of Law," caused his early followers to call him Buddha ("Enlightened One"). In it he said:

> *There are two ends which the seeker must avoid. What are they? The pursuit of desires and of the pleasure which springs from desire, which is base, common, leading to rebirth, ignoble, and unprofitable; and the pursuit of pain and hardship, which is grievous, ignoble, and unprofitable. . . .*

The Buddha urged his followers to take a middle way between the pursuits of pleasure and of self-sacrifice. Life is made up of many parts, he said. Through the movement of one or more of these parts, it inevitably changes. Therefore, it is pointless for the individual to seek permanence by aggrandizing possessions, titles, or fixed relationships. The Buddha thought that such craving is the cause of sorrow. He listed Four Noble Truths which summarized this view: 1) ". . . all the . . . components of individuality are sorrow"; 2) "Sorrow . . . arises from craving . . . ."; 3) ". . . the stopping of sorrow . . . is the complete stopping of that craving, so that no passion remains. . . ."; and 4) a Noble Eightfold Path exists to stop sorrow.

This giant figure of Gautama Buddha dominates the interior of a Nara temple.

The Eightfold Path, that part of the Four Noble Truths which leads to enlightenment, may be listed and defined as follows: Right Belief is the renunciation of worldly things and the dedication to a humanitarian faith. Right Resolve is the means by which the individual dedicates himself to the achievement of Nirvana. Right Speech enables the individual to serve as a model for others to follow. Right Conduct acknowledges the sanctity of life. Right Livelihood is a life of service rather than selfishness. Through Right Effort the individual keeps his inner self free of evil thoughts. Right Mindfulness is constant awareness that craving is pointless. Right Concentration enables the individual to be selfless in his mind and overt acts.

Before the advent of Buddhism, the major Indian religions held that except for a privileged few, the soul does not die with the individual, but is transmigrated into another living thing. The way in which the individual lives his life determines whether or not the soul will be given a higher or a lower position in the universe. Against this fatalism, the Buddha said that release from transmigration may be gained by the individual who masters himself. Universal love, friendliness, joy, and equanimity are part of this mastery. The achievement of enlightment, or paradise (*Nirvana*), is gained by annihilating that part of the self which craves—the only part that can survive the body.

Simple rituals accompanied this Buddhist doctrine. The Japanese were drawn to them. Unlike the Chinese, they had no general body of philosophy whose followers would resist the new religion. In Japan, Buddhism was accepted first by the nobility who identified it with the power of China's T'ang Dynasty. Soon they discovered another reason to favor Buddhism. The Buddhists who came from China were highly artistic. Careful workmen, their monasteries were designed and decorated with a color and movement that appealed to the austere Japanese. Moreover, much of Japanese life was a search for power and possessions. Buddhism offered compassionate relief from this quest.

Shintoism, Japan's indigenous religion, did not oppose Buddhism. The two faiths coexisted. However, in much of Japanese life, particularly in the arts, Buddhism became dominant. We will see how in the thirteenth century it spread to the masses of people. During the Nara period it was chiefly confined to the aristocracy, who encouraged the construction of many Buddhist temples and monasteries. As Buddhism spread, six major sects developed, of which two were most important.

The first, the Kusha School, was associated with the earlier Indian Hinayana Buddhists. It advocated a rigid monastic life and devoted itself mostly to philosophical speculation. The second, the Kegon School, considered the historical Buddha as an agent of the essential

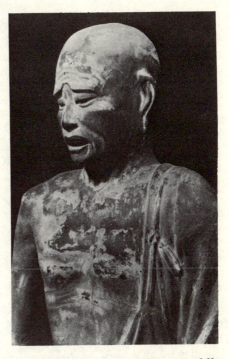

Artisans at Nara produced
this lifelike statue
of a Buddhist monk.

Buddha called Roshana, an idea rather than a man. Roshana Buddha was portrayed floating upon a lotus flower with a thousand petals— each petal representing a universe. The two schools represented the contest between the clergy and the idealists.

With the official support of the Nara government, the Buddhist schools flourished. In 749, the Emperor Shomu attended the dedication of the Great Buddha, a monument, in Nara. There he announced that grants of reclaimed riceland would be made to Buddhist missionaries. The economic position of Buddhism continued to improve as the monasteries were allowed to hold this tax-free land.

As Buddhist institutions continued to gain in wealth and influence at the imperial court, a large number of monks used their offices unscrupulously for selfish ends. The upkeep of enlarged Buddhist temples and monasteries imposed an ever greater burden on the peasantry. By the end of the Nara period, many of these institutions had become a drain on the wealth of the countryside. However, many of their monks were illiterate peasants who joined monasteries chiefly to escape the turmoil of life. Thus Buddhism gained many enemies.

Nara art. During the Nara period, architecture and sculpture flourished. Almost all works were sponsored by Buddhist institutions, and hence were religious in character.

Buddhists in the eighth century filled the temples at Nara with art such as this.

The most important achievements of Nara architecture were Buddhist monasteries. The typical monastery was a solid-framed structure, standing on a masonry terrace and crowned by a tile roof. The buildings were grouped systematically around a courtyard, entered through a formal gateway. The central building contained a large hall. Originally a pagoda was included, but it was later relegated to a site outside the courtyard. In Japan and China, the pagoda served the same purpose as the stupa in India and western Asia—it housed a relic of the historic Buddha.

One of the greatest edifices of Japanese Buddhism was the monastery of Horyu-ji (ji means "temple"). Established in 607, it included a residence and meditation center ("The Hall of Dreams") for the Regent of Japan. It was to be near this temple and other Buddhist structures that the court moved to Nara in 710. Fires have destroyed most of these buildings. Only a few have survived in their original form; but many have been rebuilt.

The Nara artisans excelled in sculpture. Whereas Chinese sculptures were usually large objects shaped in stone or marble, in Japan small bronze and woodworks were preferred. In much of their work the Japanese used lacquer. The use of lacquer was borrowed from China, but Japanese creative talent developed it to highest perfection. After discovering that the lacquer-yielding tree could be grown in the islands, Japanese sculptors devised several methods of using the liquid. One was to apply two or three layers of lacquer-soaked cloth to a solid wood frame. Another was to form a hollow mold and pour the liquid into it. The resulting lacquer figures of priests and warriors were remarkably lifelike.

CHAPTER 3

THE HEIAN ERA AND THE KAMAKURA SHOGUNATE

IN THE EIGHTH CENTURY the imperial capital was transferred from Nara to Heian, modern-day Kyoto. The reason for this move is not known, but' some historians see it as a desire to escape Buddhist clergymen who had grown powerful at Nara. Prince Naka, a leader of the Fujiwara clan had attacked the Soga leaders, who were chiefly Buddhists, and broken their power. An heir to the throne, he became the Emperor Tenji. For the next two hundred years the Fujiwara family controlled Japan.

POLITICS IN THE HEIAN PERIOD (794-1185 A.D.)

The Fujiwaras rose to power by inducing the princes of the imperial family to marry the daughters of their clan. In time, the emperor was related to the Fujiwara clan on the side of the empress. Through pressure many of the emperors were then persuaded to retire at an early age to a life of ease, leaving real power in the hands of the Fujiwara regents, called *sessho,* or civil dictators, called *kampaku.* The most famous kampaku, Fujiwara Michinaga (995-1027), was the father-in-law of four successive emperors. Under the dominance of the Fujiwara ministers, the central government extended its control over the islands of Shikoku and Kyushu, while the Ainu were pushed farther north on the island of Honshu.

As its power expanded, the Heian court became increasingly corrupt. The earlier Fujiwara leaders, such as Michinaga, Yoshifusa, and Takahira, were men of exceptional abilities, but their successors fell prey to extravagant living. In the court of Heian, frivolity and luxury prevailed. Men as well as women plucked their eyebrows, powdered and rouged their cheeks, and stained their teeth black. Courtiers passed the time writing love letters or trying to recognize the fragrance of a particular type of perfume. Other popular pastimes were costly picnics organized to watch the first blossoming of the cherry trees, or the first display of fall colors, or the appearance of the full moon each month.

Distracted by these activities, administrators paid less and less attention to affairs of state. After the tenth century, the influence of the Kyoto court in the provinces began to diminish. To meet the demands of the capital for luxuries, the peasants were saddled with

27

Heian court life was marked by elegance and formality. Here a delegation, wearing splendid robes, is being received at the entrance of the court.

additional taxes. Communications between the provinces and Kyoto broke down because the government ceased to spend money on road repairs. The conditions of anarchy in the provinces facilitated the rise of a new class of popular military aristocrats, who were soon to challenge the authority of the Kyoto government.

Economic developments. The Taiho Codes had attempted to curb private land ownership by declaring all land the exclusive property of the emperor. In 743, however, the government permitted individuals to own land if they cultivated it, but limited the size of landholdings to 1,250 acres. Some private manors, or *shoens*, were permitted to exist tax-free in exchange for political and military support. As the administration of Kyoto's government became more inefficient and corrupt, the manors grew in size. Furthermore, because the shoens were tax-free, many of the peasants turned over their overtaxed small holdings to the manor lords. These people preferred service to the lord rather than bondage to the Kyoto government, which did not even provide them with protection.

Eventually, these shoens grew to immense proportions and escaped any government control. Since the government could not control the outlying provinces, it turned power over to the various provincial aristocrats, who, in areas distant from Kyoto enjoyed almost absolute independence from the civil governors.

The Taira-Minamoto conflicts. While the Fujiwaras strengthened their grip on the imperial family, the Minamoto and Taira families, who were related to the emperor, were forced into the background. They turned to military pursuits and acquired lands away from the capital. In the long run, as the Fujiwara clan became corrupt, the Minamotos and Tairas increased their power and formed their own armies to contest the authority of the Fujiwaras.

By the eleventh century, the lords of the Taira and Minamoto families were the most powerful in Japan. The Minamoto clan was able to drive the Taira out of the Kanto Plain region. With political intrigue developing at Kyoto over the succession to the throne, court leaders invited Minamoto and Taira lords to aid their causes. Accepting these invitations, the military lords returned to the capital and replaced civilian leaders in the court.

In 1159–60, a struggle between the Taira and Minamoto factions took place in the capital. The Taira, under the leadership of Kiyomori, succeeded in killing off many of the Minamoto clan, thus obtaining control of the government. The Tairas ruled for twenty-one years. Following the pattern of the Fujiwaras, they effected marriages between their daughters and sons of the imperial family. Kiyomori had himself appointed the regent for the boy emperor. The brutality of the Taira rule led to many revolts against the regency.

While Kiyomori was embroiled in court intrigues, a survivor of the Minamoto family, Minamoto Yoritomo, rallied the remnants of his clan. In 1180, the forces of Yoritomo launched a campaign against the Taira lords. In two years Yoritomo succeeded in driving the Taira from northern Honshu. In 1185, Yoritomo decisively beat the Taira clan at the great naval battle at Dannoura. He assumed firm control of Japan.

BUDDHISM IN THE HEIAN PERIOD

As the Heian period progressed, Buddhism underwent profound changes. It became assimilated into the Japanese environment and began to lose its Chinese orientation. Further, it became aristocratic, and it did not yet appeal to the peasants. Its remoteness from the people was to continue until the end of the Heian era. Buddhist monasteries began moving from heavily populated areas to secluded retreats in the mountains. A number of conflicting sects developed during this time, of which two became important.

The Tendai sect. The sect of Tendai emphasized the existence of the historic Buddha (Gautama or Sakyamuni). It stressed the middle way between the belief in material existence and the concept that all things were an illusion. The Tendai sect held that all human beings were capable of salvation, of union with Buddha. Tendai called for a life of meditation and moral living. To provide guidance, a famous monastery, Enryakiyi, was established near Kyoto on Mount Hiei. It became the center of Buddhist learning in Japan.

The Shingon sect. The Shingon sect developed late in China and did not arrive in Japan until approximately 806. This sect dis-

tinguished between the teachings of the historic Buddha and the
"Buddha of Ultimate Reality," *Daimichi.* The latter, the "Great Illuminator," was thought to possess in his body the whole cosmos, made
up of the six elements of earth, fire, water, air, ether, and consciousness. Shingon taught that men, when free from illusion, saw the body
of the Great Illuminator even in a grain of dust or a drop of water.

Ritualism became important in Shingon. The postures,
utterances, and movements of the monks were thought to be able to
invoke certain deities. A great conflict between the Shingon and
Tendai sects developed in the Heian capital. Each developed a
private army and challenged and fought the other. A Tendai abbot,
Ennin, became a leading advisor to the royal court for twenty years.

Heian Culture

As already noted, Heian court life was largely taken up in frivolous
pursuits and a preoccupation with aesthetics. But in spite of the
prevailing dilettantism, the period also produced works of great
literary and artistic merit.

Literature. Although Chinese continued to be the language of the
noble scholars of the court, the tenth century had witnessed the
development of a native literature. It was during the Heian period
that kana, the writing adapted from the Chinese to fit Japanese
phonetics, became hiragana, or cursive writing. The credit for the
development is given to Kobo Daishi, also known as Kukai, the founder of the Shingon sect. Hiragana employed abbreviated Chinese
characters to represent Japanese sounds, an innovation which made
for greater ease in writing. Following the introduction, poetry
writing flourished among the Heian nobility. The most famous collection of poems in existence was the *Manyoshu,* a compilation of
early poets. It was prepared during the eighth century. Later, in 922,
this was incorporated into an anthology called *Kokinshu.*

The poetic style of these works was the *waka.* This verse form
consisted of thirty-one syllables, arranged in five lines of 5,7,5,7,7
syllables, without rhyme. Formal in its character, this poetic form
recognized only a restricted number of themes. In time the waka was
converted into the poetic form of *renga,* or linked verse in which one
person gave the first three lines (or 5,7,5 syllables) and another person
linked on the two remaining lines (7,7 syllables).

Heian literature reached its peak with the romantic tales called
monogatari. Unlike the brief waka poems, the monogatari ramble
on for thousands of pages. The most famous romantic narrative of
Japan is the *Genji Monogatari* (Tale of Genji). It was written between 1008 and 1020 by Lady Murasaki, using both Chinese and the
newly created hiragana. The Tale of Genji, which has been called the

first realistic novel, artfully describes the escapades and affairs of the heart of an emperor's son. The life that Lady Murasaki depicts in this monumental work faithfully mirrors that of the Heian court. Another delightful literary work of the period is the *Pillow Book* of Sei Shonagon. Together with the Genji Monogatari, it presents a complete picture of court life at Kyoto—a narrow, inbred society. Women were able to make these significant literary contributions because they were free to use kana, the writing adapted from the Chinese, while the men considered kana beneath them and wrote in the original Chinese.

Heian art. Heian religious sculpture was deeply influenced by the advent, late in the period, of a new Buddhist school, that of Amida, the "Buddha of the Western Paradise." This was, as we shall see, a popular sect which emphasized gentleness and mercy. Heian sculptors gave the Amida Buddhas a flat appearance; the treatment of the eyes (high-arching eyebrows, nearly straight upper lids and curving low lids) produced a kindly, dreamy expression.

Heian art was also remarkable for the beauty of its calligraphy. In calligraphy, the Japanese artist entered a world of pure and abstract design. Lines were set in pleasing relationships to other lines, and though a stroke might shade off from strong to light, it never faltered. By employing a varying range of color tones, from the faintest greys to the deepest blacks, Heian calligraphers produced subtle effects.

The period also witnessed the flowering of the art of making *Makimono*, or colored picture scrolls. It featured the application of gold paint to the surface of the scroll. Many makimono illustrated scenes from popular monogatari, such as the Tale of Genji.

THE KAMAKURA SHOGUNATE (1186–1333 A.D.)

With the defeat of the once-mighty Taira clan, Minamoto Yoritomo became the most powerful person in Japan. He established a military government at Kamakura, near present-day Yokohama, at some distance from the imperial court at Kyoto. In 1192, Yoritomo paid a visit to the emperor at Kyoto, and persuaded that monarch to

Genji, son of an eleventh-century emperor, was the hero of the first realistic novel. This is an old print

grant him the title of *Seii-Tai-shogun*, which means literally "Barbarian-subduing Generalissimo." There was high honor in this title although Japan was not even partly occupied or threatened by barbarians. Originally the title shogun had been granted by the emperor in times of danger from barbarian tribes, and was abolished when the threat was removed. (This practice was similar to that in ancient Rome: in times of emergency, the senate appointed a dictator for a limited period.) Yoritomo, however, received the title of shogun for life. He was granted the right to appoint his successor. Thus in Japan, the shogunate became hereditary, and an era of military rule began.

Nevertheless, the emperor still sat on his throne in Kyoto. Although stripped of all ruling power by the shogun, the emperor could not be deposed. As the direct descendant of the sun goddess, he theoretically remained the ruler of the Japanese people. All important edicts had to be issued in the name of the emperor, and one of his important functions was officially "appointing"—actually confirming—any new hereditary shogun. Thus the shogun were served by keeping puppet emperors while they were the true rulers of the country. During this period, which lasted from 1192 to 1857, the life of the emperor was in many cases pitiful. He was forced to rely upon the shogun for financial assistance. Many shogun ignored the emperors at Kyoto entirely, although they were often challenged.

The Emergence of Japanese Feudalism

During the Kamakura shogunate, the groundwork of Japanese feudalism was laid. No rigid bureaucracy existed to block its growth. This was a reversal of the pattern of China's development. We have seen that although the Chinese state periodically broke down, it never reached a permanent feudal state because certain social and environmental factors always restored the government bureaucracy. In China, the threat of nomadic invasions from Central Asia demanded a strong centralized government which had the power to raise a large army. In peacetime, the need for irrigation and flood-control projects also required centralized financing and planning. Lastly, Confucian ethics placed greater emphasis on obedience to authority than military valor, and on the knowledge of the aged than on the ambitions of the youth.

In Japan, these factors were not present. The islands did not fear foreign invasion because of their isolation from the Asian mainland. The lack of large rivers and an abundance of precipitation reduced the need for centrally managed irrigation and flood-control projects. Finally, Japan was not dominated by the Confucian philosophy, or a system of ethics comparable to Confucianism. For these reasons it could become feudalistic, whereas China always reverted to a centralized bureaucratic state.

We have noted how, during the Heian period, large shoen, or private manors, gradually built up from lands formerly owned by the emperor. Eventually, all these lands came under the patronage of court nobles or institutions such as Buddhist monasteries. Through the efforts of court nobles, many more shoen were exempted from taxes. While the court nobles pulled political strings for the shoens under their patronage, another group, the estate managers, lived on the estates and administered them for the absentee nobles. They were aided by warriors called *samurai*.

The lands of the shoen were worked by the cultivators, or *sakunin*. Their relation to the land fell into three classifications: 1) *free tenure*, whereby each cultivator owned his own tract and passed it on to his heirs without interference from the noble; 2) *commended tenure*, whereby the cultivator relinquished the title to his land to gain the noble's protection and immunity from tax payments to the government, and in return for this service the noble received certain *shiki*, or rights, to the cultivator's lands; 3) *shiki tenure*, whereby the land was owned outright by the noble who granted shiki, or rights, to the cultivators, these shiki being hereditary.

The Japanese cultivator was better off than the feudal serf or manorial tenant of medieval Europe. First, he enjoyed, under the three tenure systems, permanent rights to cultivate the land, while the European serf had no such privilege. Second, the Japanese cultivator could sell or transfer all or part of his shiki, while the European serf could not.

This early print shows poor farmers begging their wealthy landlord for mercy. They wear shabby clothing and have only ropes for their belts.

A feudal lord of the Kamakura period rides on horseback, while his retainer follows on foot. The lord carries a longbow and quiver of arrows.

By the fifteenth century, Japanese feudalism was well-advanced. Two developments during the Kamakura period aided the growth of feudalism: reconstruction of the system of tenures and the advent of the offices of the "steward" and the "constable." In the future, these officials were to become feudal lords supported by private armies.

After the founding of the Kamakura shogunate, the military government, or *bakufu*, of the shogun began to confiscate the free tenures and bind the cultivators to the other forms of landholdings. In addition, the bakufu appointed military governors, or constables, to the provinces and civil officials, or stewards, to the public and private shoens. These bakufu officials were to preserve order by maintaining an army provided for from a special tax imposed upon the nobles. These constables and stewards became the immediate vassals to the shogun, and through them allowed the bakufu an opportunity to impose their authority in regions not under their immediate control.

But although in this period Japan moved closer to feudalism, the system was not yet absolutely established. The nobles resented the appointment of the stewards to their shoen and opposed the imposition of a special tax to maintain the steward's armies. The cultivators with free tenure also asserted their right to hold land and violently opposed the confiscation of their holdings. The peasants under the nobles challenged the division of functions between constables and the stewards. In the end they paid the nobles a special tax by receiving less shiki from the lands. Finally, all groups became concerned with the constables, who began to assume greater authority over everyone. During the Kamakura period, these social innovations were still in a state of flux.

THE EVOLUTION OF JAPANESE BUDDHISM

Under the Kamakura shoguns, Buddhism changed drastically from the aristocratic cult that it had become earlier in the Heian period. It became a popular faith. These changes were the result of: 1) the decline of the Kyoto nobility; 2) the arrogance and corruption of the Buddhist clergy at Nara and Kyoto; 3) the rise of a comparatively unsophisticated military class; 4) civil wars in which danger and sudden death created a need for a simple doctrine of salvation.

Amida Buddhism: the Jodo sect of Honen Shonin. The Buddhist monk Honen Shonin was the founder of the popular Jodo, or Pure Land sect. His religion was open to all without special knowledge or training. It marked a departure from earlier forms of ritualism to a simple trust in piety. Honen emphasized the benign aspects of a deity called Amida Buddha, who had pity and mercy for all. To gain salvation, all that was necessary was to perform the *nembutsu*, repeating Amida Buddha's name with feeling and sincerity.

The Jodo sect won many converts. Though the jealousy of the Nara sects forced Honen into exile for many years, and many of his followers were put to death, his form of Buddhism continued to spread.

The Lotus sect. The greatest challenge to the worship of Amida Buddha was the religion of Nichiren, who predicted foreign invasions. Unlike other teachers, he sought to associate religion with the prosperity of the state. Nichiren denounced all other schools of Buddhism as false and detrimental to Japan. Basing his teachings upon the Lotus Scripture of the Tendai sect, he stated that for salvation man had only to invoke the name of that document.

While Amida Buddhism encouraged devotion, Nichiren's creed proposed militancy. Nichiren called Honen the "Spirit of Hell;" all Amida Buddhists were doomed and Shinshu Buddhists were traitors. Nichiren preached that governments would experience nothing but disorder until they stamped out all sects but his. As a result of his violent criticism of the government, he was driven into exile and almost murdered. Ironically, after his death, Lotus priests claimed the power to drive out evil spirits, thereby adopting the cultism he despised.

Zen Buddhism. In the tenth century the government of China, driven from the northwest by Mongols, established itself at the mouth of the Yangtze River. There, close to the sea, it was able to develop an extensive international trade. While doing so, it officially adopted what had been a provincial form of Buddhism called *Ch'an.* This word was derived from the Sanskrit word *dhyana,* meaning "meditation."

Ch'an Buddhism required profound self-discipline but not necessarily scholarship or logic. It maintained that by physical effort and concentration the individual could achieve a sudden and direct intuitive perception. It equated this achievement with enlightenment. Priests of this sect studied no sutras and performed no rituals or ceremonies. Instead, they would guide their students toward enlightenment by requiring them to concentrate completely on poetic, often irrational problems, such as, "What is the sound of one hand clapping?"

A Japanese monk named Eisai visited China early during the Kamakura period and helped to spread Ch'an Buddhism, called Zen by the Japanese, throughout Japan. Monks of the sect, fleeing from further Mongol attacks in China, later came to Japan. Their knowledge of China and of international trade quickly enabled them to become political and religious advisers to the Japanese government. The great Zen master Muso was the chief adviser to Ashikaga Takauji, a general. With Muso's help, Ashikaga Takauji succeeded in developing an enormous private trade with China. His ships brought Japanese products, such as fans and swords, and he traded them in China for precious metals and works of art. The Zen priests who managed this trade were admired throughout Japan. The military, particularly, respected Zen Buddhism because of its commercial success and its relatively simple but effective self-discipline.

KAMAKURA CULTURE

Although the political life of Japan was based increasingly at the shogun's capital at Kamakura, the cultural center was still Kyoto. The growing importance of the military and of Buddhism was reflected in the arts. Realism and simplicity showed the influence of militarism. In religious sculpture, for example, the military taste for strength and simplicity prevailed over the formal ornate style of the Heian period. Figures of the Buddhas became rounder and more robust in appearance by contrast to the earlier delicate, flat ones. Japanese sculptors began to carve muscular bodies, using realistic crystals for the eyes, and showing the heavy folds of drapery. Buddhas of the later Kamakura period expressed the rugged military life of the Kamakura shogunate. This vigorous new style also affected architecture. Monasteries and shrines were built with encircling walls, solid gates, and quarters for guards. The influence of Zen Buddhism was reflected in the austere designs and the harmony of buildings and their landscapes.

Painting. In the Kamakura period *emakimono*, or picture scroll painting, flourished. The scrolls were only ten to fifteen inches high but reached more than thirty feet in length. This form was borrowed from China. The Chinese had developed scroll painting to give a panoramic view of nature; successive mountain ranges were brilliantly shown on them, for example. The Japanese used the scrolls to describe the nature of man or to tell a tale. Heian scrolls had treated religious subjects, court scenes, or tales, and had been unrealistic in style. The scrolls of the Kamakura period were more realistic and often showed real people such as Minamoto Yoritomo, or scenes of battles and armies on the march. The various Buddhist schools usually had emakimonos illustrating the life of the founder of their sect.

POLITICAL DEVELOPMENTS IN THE KAMAKURA PERIOD

After the death of Yoritomo in 1199, the power of the Minamoto family weakened. Through Yoritomo's marriage with the daughter of Hojo Tokimasa, the Hojo family had been influential in the government. Following the death of Yoritomo, Tokimasa and his relatives obtained the position of regent to the young Minamoto shogun.

Hojo Regency (1205–1333). Yoritomo's successor to the throne was only seventeen. At first, the bakufu appointed a regency council, but after a struggle Hojo Tokimasa seized control. The emperor in Kyoto attempted in vain to wrest power from the Hojos, but his failure resulted in even more absolute control for the regent, or *shikken*, who won power by means of intrigues and assassinations. After the retirement of Tokimasa, nine members of the Hojo family successively held the office of shikken to the shogun.

Though the Hojos were usurpers, they were able administrators and strengthened the feudal system. Law under them was harsh but fair; it severely punished corruption in the government. Mindful of the corruption to which the Fujiwara regents had fallen prey, the Hojos enforced a policy of simple living at Kamakura. However, the stability of their reign was strained by natural calamities such as droughts and earthquakes which produced increasing popular discontent.

The Mongol invasions (1274–1281 A.D.). In 1268, the emperor of China, Kublai Khan, sent envoys to the "King of Japan" demanding that the Japanese submit to his authority. Although the emperor in Kyoto was alarmed, the Hojo Regency refused to capitulate to the Khan's demands. In 1274, after a year of preparation, a Mongol army of 30,000 men sailed for Kyushu in 150 Korean ships. At first the Japanese were no match for the warriors of the Great Khan, who were equipped with powerful longbows effective at 240 yards, and great catapults that they had used against China's walled cities. However, the Japanese warriors proved their mettle. After a bloody battle in the city of Hakata, the Mongols withdrew to their ships on the night of November 19, 1274. During the night a storm damaged much of the Mongol fleet. The Mongols fled back to Korea. The expedition cost Kublai Khan thousands of lives.

Later the Great Khan demanded homage again from the Japanese and again was ignored by the Hojo government. The Hojos had ordered the construction of defensive fortifications along the Japanese coasts. By 1280, Kublai Khan had conquered all of South China and, in June, 1281, sent a new Mongol army of 140,000 men swarming onto the beach of Hakata Bay in northern Kyushu. The protective seawall hindered the landing, however. The smaller Japanese craft played havoc with the larger Chinese and Korean junks. After a struggle recorded to have lasted fifty days, a great storm (undoubtedly a typhoon, called a *kamikaze* or "divine wind") once again struck. The Mongol fleet was destroyed with enormous loss of life.

The spectacular victory increased the prestige and power of religious groups in Japan. Shinto was credited with bringing the storms that broke the backs of the invasions. Buddhist clergy claimed credit for bringing help from their deities. Many Japanese accepted the viewpoint of the Buddhist monks. Having gained this prestige, the clergy demanded far greater rights and landholdings.

Conflict with the Buddhist clergy and the cost of meeting the Mongol threat impoverished the Hojo government. After 1281, the Hojos could no longer muster any loyalty or popular support to continue their control of the Kamakura bakufu. Corruption and luxurious living had penetrated Kamakura society. At this point, the emperor Go-Daigo who in 1331 was threatened with exile by the independently wealthy, arrogant shogunate, decided to attack.

This scene from an old scroll shows the Mongol invaders trying to land at Kyushu. Japanese arrows are sticking in the prows of their ships.

CHAPTER 4

THE ASHIKAGA SHOGUNATE AND THE
SENGOKU PERIOD

IN 1333 THE EMPEROR GO-DAIGO organized a movement against the
Hojo Regency. After initial reverses, he rallied a group of discontented lords for a second attempt. This time the Kamakura
bakufu sent against him a force under the command of Ashikaga
Takauji. However, Ashikaga switched loyalties to the emperor and
quickly crushed the armies of the Kamakura government. The Hojo
rulers were dispersed. All except one son of the Hojo family were put
to death.

With the collapse of the Kamakura shogunate, Go-Daigo restored
the rule of the imperial family at Kyoto. One of the emperor's first acts
was to issue an edict proclaiming the supremacy of the civilian government over the military. This policy alienated Ashikaga and other
military lords who had supported Go-Daigo's restoration. These lords
were too ambitious to accept a return to imperial rule. Aided by civilian officials, Ashikaga Takauji thereupon overthrew Go-Daigo, who
fled and established a court in exile at Yoshino in the mountains to the
south. By 1338, Ashikaga had consolidated his power around Kyoto.
He installed a puppet emperor, a rival from the other line of imperial
descent, who appointed him shogun. The hereditary emperor,
Go-Daigo, meanwhile remained in "power" at Yoshino.

THE ASHIKAGA SHOGUNATE (1338–1573 A.D.)

The Ashikaga governed from Kyoto. Unlike the Kamakura shoguns, who had taken pains to live frugally until the last days of their
rule, the Ashikaga lived in luxury and ease. Outside the capital discord was rife. For sixty years a feud raged between the puppet emperors supported by the Ashikaga and the legitimate emperor who
maintained his court at Yoshino. The two courts were finally reunited
in 1392. The Ashikaga could not muster much support from the other
clans and were continually at odds with powerful military lords in the
distant provinces or the bakufu at Kamakura.

The endless civil wars of the Ashikaga shogunate made a standing
military force necessary and resulted in the strengthening of the
warrior class. The Ashikaga period saw the appearance of powerful

The Ashikaga was a period of constant warfare. The samurai wore heavy, plated armor and fought with both swords and longbows, as this print shows.

daimyo, or feudal lords, who maintained their own armies. In the fourteenth century, these daimyo, who were the equivalent of the European barons, controlled all of Japan. Many daimyo were the former stewards who had seized control of the shoens and formed their own armies of loyal warriors, the *samurai.* Most daimyo, however, came from the ranks of the bakufu-appointed constables who had been placed in command of the provinces with the power to raise armies to maintain order for the military government.

The Ashikaga shogunate's authority was greatest under the reign of Yoshimitsu (1368-1394). Thereafter its power declined rapidly. By 1467, the Ashikaga controlled only five provinces situated near the capital of Kyoto. All other regions were under the sway of powerful daimyo who were constantly warring with each other. In 1467, there began conflicts called the Onin War, which lasted for more than eleven years. During this period of political chaos many daimyo rose and fell, and the power of the Ashikaga declined. The last Ashikaga was driven from Kyoto in 1573. The clan's authority was ended, though it kept the title of shogun until 1597.

Ashikaga Culture: The Muromachi Period (1392-1573 a.d.)

Although the rule of the Ashikaga was a time of political instability, it was also an era of considerable cultural accomplishment. In the history of art, as well as government, the period is referred to as the Muromachi, which was the name of the district of Kyoto where the Ashikaga military government (*bakufu*) was based. Extensive trade with China had enabled the Ashikaga to raise Japan's arts and technology to new heights.

The No drama. During the shogunate of Yoshimitsu, the so-called *No* (or Noh) drama became the favorite entertainment among aristocrats. Only on special occasions were the common people invited to the performance of a No play.

The No was a combination of many elements, including the *sarugaku*, or masquerade, performed by Shinto priests. It offered acrobatics, jugglery, ballad singing, and Chinese dances. The plays were written partly in prose and partly in verse. The lines were chanted in regular cadence by the actors, not sung or spoken. The chanting fell at the end of each sentence, in a manner resembling the intoning of Roman Catholic priests.

Some No plays are still performed in Japan. The traditional stage is an elevated structure about eighteen feet square. A pine tree is usually painted on the boards of the back wall. Around the three remaining open sides sits the audience. The chorus squats in two rows on the sides of the stage. The musicians sit at the back of the stage. Their instruments include a stick drum, two hand drums, and a lute.

The actors enter from a gallery at the side. The first actor to appear is the "assistant." He explains the circumstances under which the main actor will dance in the play. All No plays feature a dance, performed by the main actor in five parts with solemn gestures. Each actor may have companions accompany him. The chorus consists of eight to twelve men in ordinary dress. Their function is to chant the actor's lines when his dancing prevents him from speaking.

The No players devote years to diligent study and practice of gestures and impersonations. If an actor's part is that of an old man, he must master the actions and mannerisms of this character. Usually, in the No plays, the old man is characterized by slower move-

In the traditional No play, still performed in Japan, the actor stands on a pine stage. He is masked and richly dressed. The chorus sits nearby.

ments, which come a little after the beat of the music. In the past, all No actors were men. They learned the gestures and expressions of women.

The No dramas are noted for their elaborate costumes and masks. These latter are delicately carved wood sculptures, expressing sadness, jealousy, and ferocity. So subtle are the carvings that a slight change in the tilt of the head may express a different emotion.

Since the 1880's the No plays have been on the decline, although they are still performed under government patronage. As we shall see, in modern Japan the traditional No drama was increasingly replaced by the *Kabuki* theater, which in turn has been largely replaced by more modern forms of drama.

The tea ceremony. The tea ceremony developed in the fourteenth century under the influence of Zen Buddhism. The ceremony was (and still is) performed in simple, quiet surroundings, at small gatherings of friends who have common artistic tastes and interests. In a small chamber, bare except for a few beautiful objects, tea is prepared and drunk according to a strict etiquette. Meanwhile, conversation is restricted to such subjects as religion and aesthetics. The tea ceremony thus offered the more refined individual opportunity for withdrawal from worldly concerns. Under Yoshimitsu (1358–1408) the ceremony was the pastime of aristocrats. Later it was adopted by the samurai class. It lost its simplicity and became formal.

Art and architecture. The Ashikaga and the Zen Buddhist monks patronized landscape painting, which reached its heights with the works of Shubun and Sesshu. Like their Chinese masters, these painters were devoted to the use of bold, heavy ink lines. Their studies of natural scenery, done in monochrome, were beautifully balanced the serene, reflecting the simplicity of Zen teachings.

Architecture also showed Zen Buddhist influence. The most glorious surviving Muromachi buildings are the Golden Pavilion (*Kinkakuji*) and the Silver Pavilion (*Ginkakuji*) in Kyoto. The Golden Pavilion, an enchanting three-tiered structure, was designed and placed so as to harmonize with a garden and a pond. The pavilion's modest size and simple ornamentation harmonize delicately with the natural surroundings and show the great influence of Zen Buddhist thinking. Austere gardens became an important Japanese art form.

RELIGION UNDER THE ASHIKAGA

Continuing civil war and instability during the Ashikaga fostered the growth of popular Buddhism. At a time when life was in constant jeopardy, Buddhism's promise of salvation appealed to the masses. As it gained in power and prestige, Zen Buddhism won increasing influence at the Kyoto court, where the Tendai sect had formerly enjoyed favor. Zen's original simplicity still appealed to the samurai class, but its newly developed ritualistic and ceremonial aspects appealed to the court nobility. As it prospered, the Zen sect built large temples and monasteries at Kyoto and Kamakura.

As the rule of the Ashikaga weakened, many Buddhist sects formed their own armies. Several of them formed alliances with powerful daimyo families. The arrogance of many of these sects was demonstrated when the Tendai monks invaded Kyoto in 1470. They destroyed the temple of a rival sect. Conflicts between hostile Buddhist schools occurred throughout Japan. In the outlying provinces, followers of Nichiren clashed with numerous Buddhist sects. By the middle of the sixteenth century, most of the Nichiren temples had been destroyed, and with them the influence of Nichiren's followers. But although Buddhism remained the dominant religion during this period, Shintoism also survived. Several powerful daimyo families were followers of Shinto and continued to protect the important shrines at Ise and Izumo.

Economic Developments under the Ashikaga

Japan, under the Ashikaga, was prosperous despite warfare. The country's flourishing trade spread to China and Korea. Farmers produced more; the Hojo Regency's changes in the land laws had begun to bear fruit. Instead of practicing primogeniture, the farmers were required to will their land to all of their sons. This resulted in more farmers. With smaller land holdings, the cultivators turned to intensive farming practices. This increased productivity. In the fourteenth and fifteenth centuries the farmers organized associations that became strong enough to resist even the daimyo and the shogun.

Increasing trade led to the growth of a money economy in place of the barter system. It produced marketplaces which soon became small towns. In them, merchants and guilds (*za*) dominated the economy. By the end of the Ashikaga period they had almost complete control over the prices of rice and grains. In contrast to China, where the mercantile class never fully challenged the power of the gentry officials, Japanese merchants began to gather strength during this period. We will see how after 1700 they became one of the most influential groups in Japanese society. The significance of the success of the Japanese merchant class can be seen when contrasted with the history of mercantilism in China. The failure of the Chinese merchants to challenge the traditional values of Confucianism produced a static, antiquated system. China was unable to check the encroachment of modernized, industrial Western powers in the nineteenth century. It was because of the merchants that Japan in a brief period of forty years (1860–1900) was able to make the sudden leap from a feudal society to an industrial one.

A TIME OF WARFARE: THE SENGOKU PERIOD (1485-1568 A.D.)

The sixteenth century was a period of widespread unrest and political disintegration, referred to as the Sengoku period, or "The Age of the Country at War" (*Sengoku Jidai*). By the year 1485, powerful daimyo had carved out for themselves large domains outside the pale of Ashikaga power. On these feudal domains the daimyo were completely independent. They maintained their own armies of samurai, enforced their own laws, and squeezed taxes from the peasantry. In the early 1500's the peasants, driven to desperation, revolted frequently against their military overlords. Often these uprisings were led by local Buddhist monks of the militant Ikko movement. By mid-century many of the older daimyo families had been overthrown. New leaders, drawn from the ranks of shoen managers and peasantry, rose to power. In the second half of the sixteenth century, long struggles between a dozen new daimyo ended with the triumph of the Tokugawa family around 1600.

From their castles, the daimyo were able to control nearby villages. The villages were policed by disciplined samurai and administered by foremen whom the daimyo trained. Whoever lived in these villages survived by the grace of the feudal lords. Their rules were so harsh that a whole family might be executed if one of its members criticized the daimyo who governed it. In this time, many village industries, particularly in mining and handicrafts, were developed. There was commerce between villages, over roads built by the daimyo, but little free social activity. It was a period in which people lived in constant fear.

A crucial development of the period, which radically transformed the power struggle, was the arrival of the first Europeans in Japan. In 1542, when Japan was suffering political anarchy, Portuguese merchants arrived at the small island of Tanegashima off southern Kyushu. The Portuguese galleons brought silks and other rich wares from China and Southeast Asia. Of all their goods, those which most impressed many of the daimyo were firearms. With their limited introduction, the strategy and tactics of Japanese warfare was altered. Although the traditional weapons of war—sword, crossbow, and horse—were used extensively throughout the sixteenth century, the introduction of the lethal *"Tanegashima teppo"* (rifles imported through Tanegashima) enabled a few daimyo to rule the country.

Political developments in the Sengoku. Out of the turmoil of the century of warfare, Japan finally emerged politically integrated and stabilized to a degree unknown in earlier eras. The unification of the country was largely the work of three great daimyo: Oda Nobunaga (1534-1582), Toyotomi Hideyoshi (1536-1598), and Tokugawa Ieyasu (1542-1616). All three made use of the Western techniques of warfare. They equipped large armies of foot soldiers with firearms, against which the samurai cavalry were no match. They also built massive stone castles with breastworks for cannon which could completely command the countryside.

The first to apply the new weaponry was Oda Nobunaga. He inherited a domain from his father and associated himself with loyal allies, notably Tokugawa Ieyasu. Nobunaga defeated most of the neighboring daimyo in the vicinity of his lands at Owari on the Nagoya plain. In 1560, he gained a great victory over the powerful feudal lord of Totomi. Invited to Kyoto by the emperor, Nobunaga installed Ashikaga Yoshiaki as his puppet shogun. He had himself appointed vice-shogun, but actually held all the power. The amazing rise of Oda Nobunaga, who had been a small daimyo, alarmed other daimyo, who looked upon him as a threat. They formed alliances against the upstart, but Nobunaga routed them all.

Osaka Castle, built on a hill during the Sengoku period, was a new kind of fort. Its stone walls and breastworks were well above attacking archers.

Feeling more secure, Nobunaga turned his attentions to the powerful and hostile Buddhist forces who had aligned themselves with his opponents. The Buddhist clergy of the powerful Ikko sect, supported by the great daimyo families of Mori and Takeda, controlled large areas around Kyoto and Osaka. Nobunaga methodically assaulted and burned the Buddhist monasteries which were the main centers of power. But at the height of his power, in 1582, Nobunaga and a small band of bodyguards were surrounded. Faced with certain death, he committed suicide (*harakiri*) according to the samurai's code.

Nobunaga's ablest commander was Toyotomi Hideyoshi. He was the son of a poor peasant farmer who entered the service of the Nobunaga family at the age of twenty-two. A shrewd person, he rapidly rose in the ranks. He became Nobunaga's most trusted and brilliant general. When Hideyoshi heard of his master's death, he quickly marched to Kyoto with his army and assumed the leadership against the alliance of clergy and daimyo. Establishing his headquarters at Osaka, Hideyoshi renewed the military alliance with Tokugawa Ieyasu. By 1587, the peasant-statesman had crushed his principal rivals and emerged as Japan's most powerful daimyo.

One of Hideyoshi's first acts upon taking power had enduring importance. Even before he had complete control, in 1582, he ordered the first land survey in Japan. This task, which took sixteen years, strengthened the independent farmer and freed him from his overlord by helping to guarantee his rights to his farm. However, the survey also assisted feudalism in Japan. Through it, Hideyoshi was able to make huge grants of land to his vassals who supported him. During times of war they were required to provide him with both soldiers and up to two-thirds of their revenue from the land.

After the defeat of the daimyo-Buddhist alliance, Hideyoshi next made war against the powerful family of Shimazu. The Shimazu had dominated the region of Satsuma in Kyushu since the twelfth century. The Shimazu clan had encroached upon the domain of one of Hideyoshi's vassals, as well as having insulted the peasant leader. After initial successes by Hideyoshi's forces, the daimyo of Satsuma had no choice but to accept the peasant-soldier's terms of settlement. In return for vows of allegiance, Hideyoshi allowed the Shimazu clan to remain in power. Finally, Hideyoshi turned to western and northern Japan and by skillful diplomacy was able to bring the daimyo into his alliance. In 1588, his complete authority was symbolized by the "Sword Hunt," in which he collected thousands of weapons and melted them to make a image of the Buddha.

Hideyoshi's Korean expeditions. With Japan pacified, Hideyoshi was confronted with the problem of what to do with the vast armies at his disposal. Besides, many of his vassals were demanding land in payment for their services. Hideyoshi, though devoted to preserving

Toyotomi
Hideyoshi
(1536–1598)

the peace at home, decided to use his idle warriors in foreign conquest. In 1590, he resolved to invade China, ruled by the Ming Dynasty. He demanded safe passage through Korea for his armies. Korea, a protectorate of China, refused. Hideyoshi thereupon invaded Korea and easily overran the port of Pusan. His armies moved swiftly northward and conquered the capital of Seoul. After six weeks, the Korean government collapsed and was forced to flee north toward the Yalu River. Faced with disaster, Korea's rulers sought aid from China.

The fatal flaw in Hideyoshi's plan of conquest was his misjudgment of Korea's naval strength. The Strait of Tsushima, a strip of water 125 miles wide, separated his home base of Nagoya from the Korean mainland. Though Hideyoshi's land forces proved superior to the Koreans and Chinese, the Korean navy was far stronger than that of the Japanese. The Korean warships were of tortoise-like design, protected by iron plates and jutting spikes and equipped with battering rams. These powerful ships of Korea harassed Hideyoshi's armies and finally succeeded in cutting them off from their supply bases in Japan.

The Chinese, contemptuous of Japanese military prowess, sent an army of only 5,000 men to Korea—and were speedily crushed by Hideyoshi's army of 200,000. But denied supplies from Japan by the Korean navy, Hideyoshi was obliged to conclude a truce. The Japanese withdrew from northern Korea. They kept control of just the southern tip of the peninsula, around the port of Pusan. Hideyoshi later resumed hostilities and sent another large expedition to Korea. It achieved no lasting successes. After the death of

Hideyoshi in 1598, the Japanese withdrew from the mainland. Not until modern times did Japan once more resort to foreign conquest.

The triumph of Tokugawa Ieyasu. Hideyoshi's death left various contenders for power in Japan. One of the strongest was Tokugawa Ieyasu. In 1598, through alliances with Nobunaga and Hideyoshi, this resolute daimyo had gained vast holdings in northern Japan.

Hoping to perpetuate the rule of his family, Hideyoshi had created a board of regents to protect the rights of his five-year-old son, Hideyori. This board included Tokugawa Ieyasu. However, Hideyoshi's trust was violated, and power was subsequently split between two contending groups. One group was headed by Ieyasu, the other by an alliance of daimyo. Conflict erupted. In 1600, Tokugawa's forces defeated the alliance at the decisive Battle of Sekigahara. (Later, in 1615, the last of the Hideyoshi clan perished when Ieyasu captured and razed the castle of Osaka.) In 1603, the Tokugawa shogunate was firmly established.

RELIGIOUS DEVELOPMENTS: THE CHRISTIAN MISSIONARIES

In 1549, the Portuguese Jesuit, Francis Xavier, arrived at the port of Kagoshima with two companions. The daimyo of Kyushu, anxious to develop trade, realized that the best way to do so was to treat the Jesuits kindly. They correctly believed that good relations with the missionaries would attract Portuguese merchants to their domains.

Hideyoshi's forces invaded Korea, conquered it, and were driven out.

Xavier (later canonized a saint) established his headquarters at Nagasaki, in Kyushu. He converted its daimyo to the Roman Catholic faith. The missionaries actively participated in the silks and precious-metal trade which developed between Nagasaki and the Portuguese colony of Macao, an island in the harbor of Canton, China. In 1573, Nobunaga allowed the Christians to practice their religion openly in the capital of Kyoto. Nobunaga did not believe in Christian doctrines. Nevertheless, he was a shrewd and ambitious man, eager to learn new doctrines so that he could put them to use. His goal, inscribed on his seal, was "to bring the whole country under one sword." In addition to his interest in the knowledge of the Jesuits and the novelty of their beliefs, he saw in them able competitors for the powerful Buddhists whom he despised.

Despite their limited successes in certain areas, the missionaries were, unfortunately, overzealous. They began to display a spirit of intolerance which offended the Japanese. In 1550, Xavier was banished from Satsuma because of his opposition to Buddhism—the faith of the local Shimazu family. Elsewhere he and his brethren gave grave offense by preaching Christian doctrines which, to the Japanese, seemed to demand that they give up their traditional beliefs.

Early in Hideyoshi's reign, the Jesuits continued to receive official sanction to preach their doctrines. The Japanese were particularly interested in the Western technology brought by the Jesuits—the clocks, pianos, books, and compasses, for example. They knew that learning about this technology ultimately would bring profit. As long as Hideyoshi, like Nobunaga, could use Christian converts against the Buddhists and learn from them, he tolerated the missionaries. Once his enemies were subdued, however, he reversed his stand. In 1587, Hideyoshi issued an edict ordering all Christian missionaries to leave Japan or face execution. At the same time, he informed the Portuguese merchants that they could continue their trade only if they obeyed all Japanese laws. Hideyoshi never enforced his edict, however. His anger with the missionaries stemmed from their desire to convert. In 1588, he received a letter from the Portuguese viceroy in India, requesting safe conduct for Jesuit missionaries. Rejecting the request, Hideyoshi wrote to the Viceroy:

Ours is the land of the gods, and God is mind. Everything in nature comes into existence because of mind. Without God there can be no spirituality. Without God there can be no way. . . . In your land one doctrine is taught to the exclusion of others, and you are not yet informed of the philosophy of Humanity and Righteousness. Thus, there is no respect for God and Buddha. . . . A few years ago the so-called Fathers came to my country seeking to bewitch our men and women. . . . At that time punishment was administered to them, and it will be repeated if they should return to our domain to propagate their faith.

In 1592, Spanish merchants and Franciscan friars arrived at Kyoto from the Philippines. Hideyoshi welcomed them and accorded them the same privileges as the Portuguese merchants and missionaries. However, the Franciscans, like the Jesuits, were prohibited from holding services in Kyoto. Unlike the Jesuits, the Franciscan friars ignored the order, established a church at Kyoto, and began converting. Hideyoshi was preoccupied with his Korean adventure and at first did nothing to stop them. There were about 500,000 converts by 1615.

In 1596, an incident took place which changed the future of the missionaries in Japan. A Spanish galleon, the *San Felipe*, sought refuge from a typhoon in a port in Shikoku. The local daimyo claimed possession of both ship and cargo. The Spanish captain protested. Producing a map of the world, he pointed out the vast possessions of the Spanish monarch, who would turn his power against Japan if the *San Felipe* were not released. When asked how the king of Spain had been able to acquire such a vast empire, the captain explained: first missionaries are sent to the new lands to make converts. Soldiers follow who join with the converts in overthrowing the government, he said.

When this interview was reported to Hideyoshi, the shogun decided to act against the Franciscans who had earlier disobeyed his commands. He had six Franciscan friars publicly executed. Irritated by the increasing bickering between Franciscan friars and Jesuit priests over jurisdiction for conversion activities, Hideyoshi also ordered all Christian missionaries to leave the country. The missionaries went through the motion of packing, but most remained in Japan under the protection of their congregations. A respite was granted by Hideyoshi's death in 1598.

Thus ended the most violent period in Japanese history. Yet, in spite of its disorder, it was a period of extraordinary accomplishment. In large measure the achievements were due to Zen Buddhists. "Wherever you go, be the master," they said. They helped Japan to become involved in active trade, chiefly with China. They affected art, literature, politics, and philosophy with their concepts of restraint and practicality. Their influence during the Ashikaga Period was so powerful that some historians refer to this time as the Age of Zen Culture.

CHAPTER 5

THE TOKUGAWA SHOGUNATE: THE EDO PERIOD
(1603–1867 A.D.)

WISHING TO ESTABLISH HIS MILITARY HEADQUARTERS closer to his base in the east, Tokugawa Ieyasu founded his bakufu government at Edo, present-day Tokyo. Ieyasu was determined to make Edo the new cultural and economic center of Japan. Large tracts of land at Edo were distributed to merchants of Kyoto and Osaka to encourage their move to the new capital. At the new site in 1606, Ieyasu built a massive stone castle with money obtained from vassal daimyo.

Tokugawa Ieyasu resigned from the office of shogun in 1605 in favor of his eldest son, Hidetada. For the remaining eleven years of his life he trained his son in statesmanship. He also completed his war against the clan of Hideyoshi. In 1622, Hidetada, in turn, was succeeded by Iemitsu. This powerful shogun remained in office until 1651.

THE EXCLUSION OF CHRISTIAN MISSIONARIES AND MERCHANTS

At first, Tokugawa Ieyasu welcomed European merchants in Japan. He invited Spanish merchants to Edo in hopes of developing the commercial activities of his capital. The Spaniards and Portuguese declined because of the distance. Tokugawa concluded that the Spanish were more interested in making converts to Catholicism than in promoting commerce.

By the end of the sixteenth century, the Dutch and the English were beginning to break Portugal's monopoly on the Asian trade. In 1600, a Dutch ship, the *Liefde*, arrived in Japan. Its English captain, Will Adams, became a close adviser of Tokugawa Ieyasu. He taught him the arts of shipbuilding and navigation. He also warned the shogun of the expansionists designs of European nations. Like the Portuguese, the Dutch and English chose to trade at the southern ports of Kyushu. Tokugawa encouraged the daimyo of Kyushu to build ships and take part in the commerce with China and Southeast Asia. Thus a rivalry began between Japanese and European merchants.

In the final battle of Osaka (1615), which pitted the last remnants of Hideyoshi's supporters against the forces of the Tokugawa, many Japanese Christians sided with Hideyoshi's son, Hideyori. This

provoked the enmity of Tokugawa Ieyasu and his son. After the anni-
hilation of the Hideyoshi clan, the shogun ordered all Christian
missionaries to leave Japan. Because of the presence of English and
Dutch merchants, it no longer seemed necessary to tolerate the
Portuguese and Spanish. The religious orders from these countries
had, after all, shown their inability to live together. They had involved themselves in struggles in which they occasionally exchanged
commercial advantages for the promise of converts.

Tokugawa Ieyasu did not want to take the chance that some of his
officials might become Christians. He ordered the execution of all
Christian missionaries who refused to leave. A few of the missionaries
stayed on and perservered despite persecution.

The persecutions were continued by Tokugawa Iemitsu
(1622–1651). By 1636, the Spanish and English had departed from
the islands. The Portuguese were restricted to their base at Nagasaki.
There, trade with the West flourished. After the death of a local
daimyo from Nagasaki in 1637, a force of 37,000 impoverished
peasants and unemployed samurai, most of whom were Christians,
seized control of an old castle on the Shimabara Peninsula near
Nagasaki. The Christian rebels aided by the guns of Dutch ships,
defied a besieging army of more than 100,000 men for more than two
months. Then their supplies and food gave out. While the uprising
was primarily an expression of the intolerable living conditions of the
times, the Tokugawa rulers suspected that it had a religious basis. All
but a few of the rebels were subsequently executed. With this
massacre organized Christianity in Japan, which had always been
limited, was prohibited. Some "hidden Christians" remained to
pursue their work, however.

Following the rebellion, Iemitsu further restricted contact with
the Western powers. He prohibited all Japanese from leaving their
homeland and banned construction of ocean-going vessels. He
decreed that any Japanese living overseas who returned home would
be executed. In 1639, the Portuguese merchants were banished and,
in 1640, only the Dutch remained. After 1641, Dutch agents were
confined to the small island of Deshima in Nagasaki Bay. They were
held almost as prisoners. Only a few European ships, those of
Holland, were allowed to dock at Deshima each year.

From 1640 to 1854, Japan was practically isolated from the rest of
the world. The consequences of this self-enforced isolation were
far-reaching, both on the domestic and international levels. Japan's
seafaring days of the fifteenth and sixteenth centuries were ended.
She would no longer be in a position to establish colonies in the
Pacific—to change the course of Western imperialism. Japan had
internal reasons for this policy. The central government wanted to
control daimyo who stood to profit from trade with the West. By

Tokugawa Ieyasu (1542–1616) at first welcomed Western merchants, but later banished them from Japan.

eliminating international trade, these daimyo would be deprived of income and of potential alliances with foreigners. Moreover, Japan feared religious subversion by the Western missionaries. For the next two hundred years she kept her door closed to the West. During these two centuries, Deshima was the only crack through which the Japanese might catch a glimpse of Western thought and technology.

Administration and law. With the development of the Tokugawa shogunate, Japanese feudalism reached a final, "centralized" stage. Governing power was at Edo. The emperor was maintained at Kyoto as a figurehead. This system, which preserved the ancient form of rule while giving real control to the shogun, was first perfected by Tokugawa Ieyasu. All vassal daimyo were divided into groups. One, the *fudai* daimyo, or hereditary lords, consisted of members of the Tokugawa clan and its most loyal vassals. To these daimyo Ieyasu granted lands close to Edo and in the areas of Kyoto and the Kanto Plain. The fudai were situated so as to guard the military capital from attack. A second group was made up of the *tozama* daimyo, or "outside" lords. These included the powerful lords Shimazu of Šatsuma, Date of Sendai, and Maeda of Kanazawa. The tozama were made to remain in the outlying districts, in such a manner as to prevent them from forming alliances with each other. Spies were sent to each domain to report on the activities of each daimyo and his samurai. If the shogun concluded that a daimyo was not fulfilling his duties or was plotting against the government, he would confiscate the suspect's domain or transfer him to another region.

Both the fudai and the tozama were obliged to pledge loyalty to the Tokugawa shogunate. The Shogun decreed that only the fudai daimyo could hold important bakufu positions. Chief cities and check points along main highways were put under the control of loyal vassals. This strategy offset the offensive power of the tozama, who were individually richer than the fudai and so required forceful action to contain.

Under Tokugawa Iemitsu, the tozama were even more tightly controlled. He enforced a system called the *sankin-kotai*, or "alternate attendance." Each tozama lord was required to spend several months at Edo on a regular basis. When he returned to his own estate, he was obliged to leave his wife and children at the capital as hostages. The enormous cost of transporting their families and staffs depleted the wealth of the tozama. For many of them, the high costs of city life helped to complete their impoverishment. To thwart the formation of hostile coalitions, the government also reserved for itself the right to approve marriages between daimyo families. In addition, it prohibited the tozama from strengthening the defenses of their castles. At the same time it demanded that they contribute money and manpower to the construction of projects wanted by the central authorities—fortresses, bridges, and roads.

The early Tokugawa rulers were faced with the task of bringing peace and order to a society that had long been at war. The philosophy of Neo-Confucianism, imported from China, became the basis for their efforts to establish a new political ideology. The Tokugawa administrators based many of their decrees on the Confucian tenet that there is a natural order to the universe. They passed laws which defined a class order and prescribed the type of behavior expected of each class member—samurai, peasant, and merchant alike. The feudal lords and their retainers (vassals and

Obedient to Tokugawa Iemitsu, Tozama lords traveled regularly to Edo to live near the court. The expensive journeys tended to weaken them.

samurai) were required to divide their time between the study of literature and warlike sports and exercises. A strict code of behavior called *Bushido* ("Way of the Warrior"), helped to guide the samurai by giving them a model for conduct. They were called upon to be loyal and unquestioning to their superiors, ever ready to face any hardship in the name of duty. The code forbade drunkenness, ostentation, and licentiousness. It encouraged respect and obedience, values long emphasized in Japanese society.

The Tokugawa did not formulate a comprehensive legal code, but made laws to deal with situations as they developed. Special behavior was prescribed by the Bushido code of ethics. Originally a feudal code of loyalty between lord and vassal, by the middle of the Tokugawa period it was developed into a separate ethical code to cover relations between all classes: peasant and merchant, merchant and clerk, farmer and laborer, and artisan and pupil. Placards proclaiming the correct mode of behavior between men and women, parents and children, and older and younger children were conspicuously displayed throughout towns and villages. Peasants were admonished to be frugal and to work hard, to get up early, and to consume less rice and no tobacco. Like many other fixed rules, the Bushido and its related codes did not have the flexibility to change as the society changed. Thus often they were self-defeating. In order to attain control, the Tokugawa passed laws designed to tie the peasants to the land. The ineffectiveness of these laws was attested by the large migration from rural areas to the cities during the period.

The effort to control the samurai was another example of an adverse affect of the Bushido. As more and more of the samurai were persuaded to become scholars, they rediscovered the ancient Japanese traditions and the religious tenets of Shinto. They thus became aware of the divine ancestry of the imperial family and came to believe that the emperor was not only the source of political power, but also was entitled to exercise it. By the beginning of the nineteenth century, many samurai were loyal to the emperor. They were the cause of a "Shinto Renaissance" which was a harbinger of the fall of the Tokugawa.

During the Tokugawa period, lawbreaking was severely punished, for the Tokugawa believed that a fear of harsh retribution would deter crimes. The heads and trunks of decapitated criminals were publicly displayed. Sometimes criminals were buried to their waists. Passers-by were encouraged to carve them with bamboo saws. Arsonists, when caught, were burned alive. Like the knights and serfs of medieval Europe, the samurai and commoners were punished differently for similar crimes. Members of Japan's lowest class could be put to death merely for "rude" behavior. A samurai, whose class was close to the top of the social order enjoyed certain privileges which those below did not share. One of these was the right of *kirisute gomen*. This permitted him to use his sword to "cut down" a commoner who was disrespectful, and then continue on his way.

THE ROOTS OF CHANGE IN TOKUGAWA JAPAN

Economic life. The Tokugawa shogunate, in bringing peace to Japan, benefitted the merchant, or chonin class, most of all. Once feuding domains were brought under control, production increased and trade became more widespread. Many barriers which feudal lords had set up to tax passing merchants were eliminated by the central government. Roads and communications were improved. Currency was standardized. But although the central government helped the merchants to become more independent, it was not ready to grant them freedom from all restraints.

To control the chonin, the government encouraged them to settle in cities where its power was supreme, Osaka, Kyoto, and Edo. Similarly, daimyo asked the merchants of their domains to move to castle towns where their services were needed. The merchants and artisans prospered in the rapidly developing areas to which the daimyo and samurai flocked to buy their wares—clothing, weapons, and other goods. Eventually the old bartering system, whereby rice served as a medium of exchange, became too cumbersome. In the larger centers of trade, the use of money became prevalent during the Ashikaga period. By the end of the seventeenth century, all of Japan had shifted to a money economy.

The merchants won favor because they assumed functions and performed services which were indispensable to the ruling classes. The samurai class was less lucky. By the end of the fighting, as the Tokugawa shogunate progressed, the samurai found themselves idle and restless. They were appeased with regular pensions or stipends of rice, which were drawn from the farmlands of their lords' estates and which they used for barter. In many instances, the daimyo also had to provide land for their retainers to live on. As in the past, the samurai class was sustained by the sweat of the Japanese peasants. The

Two centuries after its perfection by masters, Japanese "Floating World" (*Ukiyo-e*) woodblock printing lives on. This is a modern craftsman.

peasants were forced to turn over a large share of their rice crops in the form of taxes paid to the samurai, daimyo, and central government.

The samurai, eager for luxury goods, began to buy on credit, pledging their future rice income. Sharp-witted merchants were quick to lend them money in return for a share of their rice stipends. While the merchants became richer serving as rice brokers and money lenders, the samurai fell deeper into debt. Gradually the chonin gained control of the rice market and began speculating. The rice brokers often drove prices so high that the samurai, whose stipends were fixed, could not buy it back. Government efforts at price controls were usually unsuccessful. When the central government tried to prevent monopolistic practices, it often found itself opposed by a strong *nakama*, or trade association.

TOKUGAWA CULTURE

The chonin class, having suddenly become rich, gained a taste for extravagant living and the arts. Although the Tokugawa shogun favored frugality and denied the merchant class the privilege of wearing silks, the chonin found ways to flaunt their new wealth. Men wore somber-looking robes, but lined them with exquisite materials. Their wives wore plain outer garments, but their underclothing was cut from the finest silks. In Osaka and Edo, which escaped the harsh military rule of the military areas, the chonin displayed their finery more openly.

Painting: the Ukiyo-e school. In the Sengoku period and during the early years of the Tokugawa shogunate, Japanese painting served aristocratic tastes for restrained elegance and morality. But as the influence of the wealthy chonin made itself felt, Japanese art became more sensuous and down-to-earth. Whereas earlier styles were Chinese-inspired, Tokugawa painting returned to ancient native techniques. Subtle gradations of tone, characteristic of Chinese painting, gave way to precise outlines. The Chinese element of atmospheric depth began to disappear. It persisted only in the treatment of mountain scenes.

Utamaro Kitagawa (1753–1806) was one of the many Ukiyo-e school painters who sought to portray everyday life in Japan. These scenes are near Kamakura.

The most famous style of this period was the *Ukiyo-e,* "Floating World Prints." The Ukiyo-e painters depicted the transient, passing scenes of daily life—the merry round of the restaurants, theaters, and brothels of the great cities. Popular dancers, actors, and courtesans were shown in brilliant costumes. These scenes of life in the bawdier quarters of town, though scorned by the upper classes, appealed to the pleasure-seeking chonin class.

The Ukiyo-e school broadened its appeal to the masses through the medium of woodblock prints. Ukiyo-e printmaking was started by an embroiderer, Moronobu Hishikawa. He fashioned beautiful wood-cuts from which inexpensive monochrome prints were made. The subjects were everyday amusements and pleasures. The best-known prints are of celebrated courtesans and actors. The first great poly-chrome printer-designer was Harunobu Suzuki. Beauty of line, of sentiment, and of color characterized his style. His ability has seldom been duplicated.

Though Ukiyo-e printing flourished well into the nineteenth century, its peak was reached late in the 1700's with the works of Kiyomitsu Torii, Utamaro Kitagawa, and Kiyonaga Torii. After 1800, Hokusai Katsushika became renowned for his landscape prints; one of the most famous, "Waves," shows huge breakers rearing up toward Mount Fuji. Like others of his day, he depicted the daily lives of the people. Working in Edo, he showed laborers fighting in the streets, women caring for their children, and samurai participating in sports contests. Hiroshige Ando, another Ukiyo-e master of the nineteenth century, is noted for his nature scenes and for prints depicting travelers along the Tokaido Road.

Tokugawa literature. The literature of Tokugawa Japan was pop-ular rather than aristocratic. One noted author of the period, Ihara Saikaku, wrote short stories about the day-to-day experiences of townsfolk. Most of his tales were frank and earthy, dealing with the amorous adventures of merchants, rogues, and bawds. One favorite short story, called in part, "The Millionaires' Gospel, Revised Version," tells to what great lengths a certain merchant would go to build his fortune. Two other famous tales by Ihara are "The Man Who Spent His Life at Love-Making" and "Five Women Who Loved Love."

During the period, a new form of poetry was created. To replace the thirty-one syllable waka, the Japanese evolved the *haiku* which consisted of only seventeen syllables. Although originally devised by the courtiers as a kind of "parlor game," the haiku was perfected as a literary form by the poet Basho Matsus (1644–1694).

The Zen Buddhist idea called *satori,* which means "Sudden

Enlightenment," affected Basho and many other writers of his time. This idea suggested that deep and extended concentration may gather in a soul and suddenly flash like lightning over the events of a lifetime, bringing a profound wisdom to its conceiver. To express this concentration leading to enlightenment, Basho and others chose the form of *haiku*. This revealed only the purest feeling, simply contained in seventeen syllables. Haiku, like the Buddhism that it represents, shows the world to be a quickly vanishing dream. Basho, the son of a poor samurai, wrote of nature. He also used his talent to criticize Tokugawa society. Basho was appalled by the careless, spendthrift ways of the city dwellers. He sympathized with the extreme poverty which often caused peasants to abandon their children. Basho wrote (in poetry that does not always have the seventeen syllables in English translation):

> *Ah, the first, the gentlest fall of snow:*
> *Enough to make the jonquil leaves bend low.*

And,

> *Deepen, O cuckoo in the wood, my mood of*
> *mutability, my solitude. . . .*

And,

> *Even a horse is a spectacle;*
> *I cannot help stopping to see it on morning snow.*

And, his most famous,

> *Breaking the silence of an ancient pond,*
> *A frog jumped into the water—a deep resonance.*

Issa (1763–1828) was another influential poet who used his works to poke fun at the class divisions of Tokugawa society. He wrote:

> *Out there a daimyo*
> *Drenched to the skin*
> *And I by the fireside.*

The popular stage: kabuki. While the samurai cultivated the No drama, the townspeople developed a dramatic form of their own, the kabuki. By the mid-1700's this popular drama was well advanced. Like the Italian opera, it combined words, music, and acting in one brilliant art form. Yet it differed from opera in many ways.

Kabuki playwrights borrowed from many existing forms, such as the *bunraku*, or puppet shows, to create performances that would appeal to a vigorous people. Their work was essentially realistic, with costumes and stage sets familiar and understandable to all. Unlike the

No players, kabuki actors did not use masks or special symbolic gestures. Rather, they declaimed, postured, and grimaced naturally and with great gusto. The townspeople demanded noise, movement, and thrills in the form of magnificent settings and costumes. Kabuki provided them all.

The greatest kabuki dramatist was Chikamatsu Monzaemon. Although he wrote for the puppet theater, his works were easily adapted to the kabuki stage. His themes were usually the conflicts between friends or lovers, and their families or society. The plays often ended with the triumph of morality and the lovers committing suicide.

THE DECLINE OF THE TOKUGAWA SHOGUNATE

While Japan's cities thrived and their merchants grew rich, the rural daimyo and the samurai did not fare well. The central government and the rural daimyo were forced to reduce the rice stipends paid to their retainers. Some daimyo, deeply in debt to moneylenders, were obliged to turn their retainers loose. These masterless samurai, called *ronin*, became dangerous. They brawled in the towns and murdered innocent people. At harvest time they raided villages and seized the rice crop. In the 1770's, this new ronin class led a number of peasant revolts and became a serious menace to the Tokugawa government.

Many samurai were unable to adjust to the increasingly commercialized economy brought about by peace. Some of the poorest of them gave up their positions and became members of the peasant class. Others were forced to turn to the once-despised occupation of the merchants to earn a living. Still others crossed class lines to marry the daughters of wealthy chonin. By 1850, the once-coveted rank of samurai could be bought. Many proud old warriors were forced to pawn their swords. (It was said that the samurai could no longer "cut down" the merchants because they had to "cut down" their expenses instead.) Those samurai who managed to cling to their positions were confused and angered by a social order which did not value their abilities.

At the lowest level of the economy, the peasantry formed the productive base of the Tokugawa society. It was controlled by daimyo through village headmen and five-family groups called *gonin-gumi*. Through this network the peasants paid their taxes and labored on public works projects. Although a few peasants prospered during this era, most lived in poverty. They depended upon landowners, some of whom had been samurai, for all of their needs.

Peasant rebellions occurred with increasing frequency during the second half of the nineteenth century. Like the daimyo and samurai, the peasants were deeply in debt to the chonin. In order to pay their loans, the daimyo taxed the peasants more heavily. Many peasants, overburdened with debts and taxes and often on the verge of starvation, were forced to mortgage their holdings. The impoverished farmers could no longer support children and often resorted to abortion and infanticide. By 1750, these practices had become common. The government strove without success to prohibit them.

Many peasants or their children fled from their farms to the cities. Others succeeded in gaining the protection of the larger tozama daimyo. The tozama usually guarded their lands and protected their peasants against the abuses of the moneylenders. They paid them allowances for raising large families.

Despite the suffering and widespread resentment that had developed because of social change, the benefits of the Tokugawa peace were evident throughout Japan. In general, over the two-hundred-year period of the shogunate, productivity and income had increased. Crops were diversified and handicraft industries were developed. But there were signs of discontent in society. The tozama lords such as Satsuma, Choshu, Hizen, and Tosa, who had developed small industries on their estates and thus enjoyed considerable wealth, waited eagerly for an opportunity to turn the Tokugawa out. The lesser vassals and the samurai were desperate for money. Among small merchants, peasants, and townspeople, resentment was boiling up against the Tokugawa and the wealthy chonin rice-brokers. Meanwhile, scholars were eagerly studying Western ways from books smuggled into the country by the Dutch. As the century advanced, the internal pressure for change became irresistible.

External Pressure: The End of Isolation

Late in the eighteenth century, the Russians had crossed the barren wastes of Siberia and reached the Pacific. Attempts to open trade with Japan failed, but Russian settlements in the Kuriles and Sakhalin Island posed a new threat to the Tokugawa. After the end of the Napoleonic Wars in Europe (1815) Britain and other Western nations showed renewed interest in Far Eastern trade. American merchants were also beginning to participate in trade with the countries of Asia.

Before 1850, Western efforts to promote trade were aimed primarily at China. When California joined the Union in 1850, United States interest in trade with the Orient increased. American sailors, shipwrecked in Japan, used to be jailed and subjected to abuse. Repeated efforts to resolve these problems and open trade negotiations with the Japanese were rebuffed by the Tokugawa government. However, after the Anglo-Chinese War of 1840 (the "Opium War"), and the opening of China to commerce, the Western powers became more insistent on trading rights being made available.

Increasingly involved in competition for overseas trade, the United States viewed its expansion to the West as essential—a fulfillment of its "Manifest Destiny." Its interest in the Orient was not limited to a desire for economic gain or for political power. Many Americans believed that Western culture and material benefits should be brought to the less developed areas of the world.

Finally the United States, which badly needed a coaling station in Japan for its ships, decided to wait no longer. In 1853, Commodore Perry, in command of a squadron of four ships, entered Tokyo Bay. The Japanese had been warned by the Dutch that the Americans were on route. But they were awed and frightened by Perry's steamships (never before seen in Japan) which puffed smoke from their stacks. Perry demanded that the Japanese open their ports to trade. He then withdrew, promising to return early in 1854 to receive an answer.

As word of Perry's visit spread through Japan, many people panicked. Some moved quickly to the countryside. Samurai were seen dragging out their old, rusted suits of armor and buttressing their castle defenses. At the beginning of the Tokugawa shogunate Japan could have resisted any invader. By the time of Perry's visit, any Western power could have forced her door ajar.

The Tokugawa government was caught in a dilemma. The emperor and conservative court officials demanded the maintenance of isolation. The Tokugawa realized, however, that Japan was helpless before the modern military might of the West. In an unprecedented move, the shogunate's leaders sought the advice and support of

This well-known Japanese print shows Perry's "Black Ship" entering Tokyo Bay in 1853. The warlords of Japan are rushing to prepare their defenses.

daimyo throughout the realm. The anti-Tokugawa tozama daimyo recognized the impossible position of the bakufu. They criticized the central authorities for taking a lenient position toward the Western intruders. Despite the accusations, the Tokugawa government had no choice but to submit to Western demands. When Perry returned, a treaty was signed on March 31, 1854. It granted the United States the rights of trade at two ports, the right of coaling and replenishing her ships, and the privilege of sending a consul within eighteen months, who would reside in the port of Shimoda.

Once the door to the West had been opened a crack, there was no closing it. Within two years, Japan was obliged to sign treaties with Britain, Russia, and Holland. In 1856, Townsend Harris, the first American consul, arrived. In two years, after much harassment and postponement, he concluded a full commercial treaty with Japan. This treaty flung the Japanese door wide open. United States citizens were granted the rights of extraterritorality in five ports. The right of residence in Osaka and Edo and the privilege of unrestricted trade also were granted. Tariffs were to be determined jointly by American and Japanese officials. The privileges of this treaty, signed by Harris, were also extended automatically to the other nations, under the "most-favored nation" clause which all Western powers had included in their treaties with the Tokugawa government.

The conservative elements of Japan assailed the Tokugawa for submitting to the West. The cry *"Sonno joi"* ("Revere the emperor—expel the barbarians!") was heard throughout Japan. Another was *"Isshin"* ("Restore the past"). Satsuma and Choshu daimyo attacked foreign vessels in their waters. Europeans were murdered on the highways. Finally, the Western powers decided to take action against Satsuma, and in 1863, a British squadron bombarded the port of Kagoshima. This military display enraged the local daimyo, who called for the expulsion of all Westerners from Japan. The central government was barely able to function under the strain. As the shogunate proved unable to deal with the crisis, other political powers moved into the leadership. By 1866, the samurai of Choshu, Satsuma, Tosa, and Hizen, probably supported by rich merchants and some peasants, formed an alliance. Their goal was to advance the cause of the emperor.

In 1867, a new Tokugawa shogun came to power. In October of that year a memorial, presented by the Tosa, Satsuma, Hisen, and Choshu daimyo, urged the shogun to surrender the reins of government to the Emperor Mutsuhito (age 14) in the interest of national welfare. To the astonishment of all, the shogun submitted his resignation to the emperor on November 2, 1867. Thus, with little bloodshed, the Tokugawa shogunate came to an end.

CHAPTER 6

MODERN JAPAN: THE MEIJI RESTORATION (1868–1912)

FOLLOWING THE COLLAPSE OF THE Tokugawa Shogunate and the restoration of imperial authority, Japan entered an era of radical change. The period of the Emperor Mutsuhito's reign is known as the *Meiji*, which means "enlightened rule." The capital was transferred to Edo, which was renamed Tokyo ("eastern capital"). Within the short span of thirty years, Japan was transformed from a decentralized feudal state into a modern industrial state.

Although Emperor Mutsuhito officially assumed supreme power, he was surrounded by advisers. They were an influential and skilled group of samurai administrators and court officials hostile to the earlier Tokugawa regime. The emperor and his advisers were determined that Japan should not suffer China's fate. The Chinese scholar-officials were strongly opposed to the introduction of Western ideas and institutions which would spell the end of their monopoly of learning and power. Yet, at the same time, China's military weakness forced her to make extensive territorial and economic concessions to the West.

Japan, on the other hand, was a society in which military virtue had long been preeminent. During the Tokugawa period, the country was controlled by military men who became bureaucrats. The leading daimyo of the bakufu resisted Western influence, fearing that it would jeopardize their authority. However, other samurai had opposed the shogun, and, in a resurgent nationalistic fervor, rallied to the side of the emperor. This group of new military leaders, unlike the Chinese Confucian scholars, realized that by borrowing from the West they could both preserve their own position and guard against Western encroachment.

Thus, while China clung to her past traditions and lapsed into semicolonial status, Japan in the Meiji period turned to the West. She speedily adopted those scientific and industrial techniques which enabled her to maintain her independence.

THE MEIJI REFORMS

The enormous task of transforming Japan from a feudal to a modern state was not accomplished overnight. Unlike the American and French revolutions, the Meiji Restoration was not motivated by such ideals as equality, liberty, and fraternity, nor by the Marxian theory of class struggle. The Japanese Restoration leaders were hard-headed, practical men whose creed was summed up in the phrase *"Fukoku kyohei"* ("rich country, strong arms"). They understood that the strength of the West lay in its industrial and military establishments. Even more, they envied the centralized constitutional forms of government which promoted national unity.

After 1869, these modern-minded reformers, anxious to put an end to foreign privileges of extraterritoriality and "most favored-nation" treatment, launched Japan on a race to catch up with the Western countries. But before these aims could be achieved, the obsolete feudal structure had to be dismantled.

Social reform: the abolition of feudalism. The first goal of the Meiji leaders was to resurrect the power and status of the emperor. To accomplish this the political strength of the daimyo and their samurai vassals had to be broken; strong central control had to be established. In 1869, the four powerful daimyo of Satsuma, Choshu, Hizen, and Tosa surrendered their domains to the emperor.

Unless their act is seen in the light of the crisis facing Japan, it is difficult to understand why the four most powerful daimyo were persuaded to show their loyalty in this way. The authority of the central government was increasingly powerful. The payment that each daimyo received for surrendering authority helped to free him from the financial problems long associated with his position. The central government assumed responsibility for his outstanding debts. To preserve the social status of the great feudal lords and court nobles, the government awarded the daimyo large pensions and titles in a newly created peerage, with five ranks from prince to baron.

Samurai such as these found themselves unemployed after the Meiji Reforms.

Yet, to these inducements there must be added another: there is in the Japanese tradition a strong desire to preserve the nation, even at the cost of personal loss. By 1871, almost all of the feudal estates had passed under the emperor's control. The former fiefs, numbering roughly three hundred, were converted into seventy-two prefectures, or ken. Three metropolitan districts were also created.

But governmental reorganization was only the first step. The upper class could safely be allowed to retain some titles. The major barrier to sweeping social and economic reforms remained the feudal distinctions between warrior, merchant, artisan, and peasant. In 1869, the first laws were passed aimed at wiping out inequalities between the traditional social classes. All persons below the rank of samurai were classified as commoners. Shortly thereafter, commoners were given the right to choose their occupation and to reside wherever they wished.

One of the most difficult problems was that of the huge samurai class, which numbered some 2,000,000. In 1871, the government abolished the special privileges of the samurai. They were even forbidden to wear their special hairdo and the two swords which had been the emblem of their class. The unemployed samurai were paid off with pensions and, later, nonconvertible government bonds. A law, introduced in 1873, established universal military conscription. This tended to reduce the power of the samurai class by depriving it of its chief role in Japanese society. In 1876, the government felt strong enough to commute all pensions, which were draining its resources. Former samurai who had not shifted their pensions into bonds were compelled to do so. This requirement was a severe blow to the samurai class. Many great daimyo and courtiers had successfully weathered the transition from feudalism. They had invested their cash in industrial projects. But many of the samurai, unskilled in money matters, had squandered and lost their holdings. Their resentment soon boiled over in futile revolts against the government.

Meanwhile, in the early 1870's other vital social reforms were enacted. They resulted in part from government policies aimed at tax reform, army building, and industrial expansion. Another purpose for them, however, was the central government's wish to gain a better position from which to negotiate with the West. Discrimination was ended against the lowest Japanese class, the *Eta*. Like the Indian Untouchables, it was made up mostly of tanners, scavengers, and other menials. By law, all men were declared free to pursue any vocation. Restrictions on travel between provinces were abolished.

Not all reforms were readily accepted by every class. The rural peasants, in particular, protested the dissolution of the *Eta*, the taxation, rising prices, and concentration on industrial expansion.

This contemporary French cartoon shows Prince Ito worshipping his idol, Bismarck. The Meiji reformers were accused of copying too much from Prussia.

They showed their dissatisfaction with social change in a number of uprisings. However, they proved no real threat to the central authorities, and the reforms continued.

In sum, the Meiji Restoration may be seen as a political movement developed in response to the challenge of the West. Although the Tokugawa shogunate might have led the country towards industrialization, it had been unable to unite all of the daimyo. The emperor was required to achieve that goal.

The modernization of Japan is often viewed as a break with the past and a borrowing from the West. It may also been seen as the extension of a Japanese value system which existed as early as the Yamato clan period and which persists today. Under this system, the loyalty of individuals is linked to primary groups, which are linked in turn to the emperor. As part of this pyramid-shaped hierarchy, the individual works loyally for collective goals. He subordinates his own needs and desires to the duties required by his position. His group strives to improve its position with respect to other groups. At times this stimulates factionalism and works against social change or material progress. At other times, it contributes to astonishing national development.

Military and industrial expansion. In 1873, the Imperial Army was created, based upon universal conscription. This important reform, which undermined the basis for the existence of a hereditary warrior class, was the work of the former Choshu samurai, Yamagata

Aritomo. Yamagata had been sent to Europe to study the organization and tactics of the French and Prussian armies. Japan's national army was closely modeled after the Prussian forces. The Japanese were especially impressed by the ease with which the Prussians defeated the French in the Franco-Prussian War (1870–1871).

Under the leadership of Ito Hirobumi and Iwakura Tomomi, far-reaching economic reforms were introduced. Ito, Iwakura, and other advisers of the emperor had traveled abroad to familiarize themselves with the ways of the West, where they also sought to negotiate an end to "unequal treaties." In the United States, England, France, and Prussia, they learned about Western industrial organization, government administration, and communication techniques. In Prussia they had an audience with Bismarck and heard him warn that a nation's material power was the ruling factor in international relations. The so-called Iwakura Mission returned home filled with ambitious plans to heed Bismarck's advice.

While these leaders were abroad, the government in Tokyo had become increasingly sympathetic with Japan's discontented samurai. Saigo Takamori, a powerful political figure from Satsuma, suggested that the warriors could be employed if Japan were to invade Korea. In 1872, a Japanese envoy went to Korea to negotiate a treaty for the opening of that "Hermit Kingdom." When he was rebuffed and insulted, Saigo demanded an invasion of Korea, both to preserve Japan's honor and to provide work for the distressed samurai.

It was about this time that the Iwakura Mission returned home. Its leaders were convinced that the country's primary concern should be the development of domestic industry. Faced with a choice between the two policies, the government ruled in favor of industrial

After the Meiji Restoration, new industries were established in Japan. Here a Western manager oversees women working in a modern textile factory.

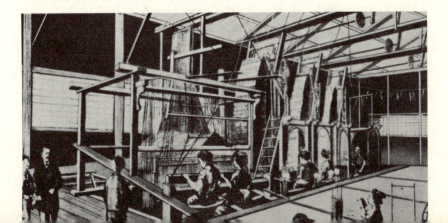

development and against the expansionist policy. Saigo was forced to resign from the government. Ito and Iwakura thus were more influential than ever.

Nevertheless, the political struggle continued. Finally, in 1877, a rebellion broke out in Satsuma. It was led by Saigo Takamori, at the head of a formidable army of trained samurai. The insurrection put the new national army, recently formed by Yamagata, to its first major test.. The army of conscripts rose magnificently to the challenge and crushed Saigo's samurai forces. The victory of the Japanese Imperial Army, made up of soldiers from all social classes, shattered the legend of the invincibility of the old warrior class. After the Satsuma Rebellion, no further revolts disrupted the plans of the central government.

Ito and Iwakura then proceeded to carry out their reform program. They acted to establish a uniform currency and to insure steady government revenues. For the latter purpose, a money tax was instituted, based on the value of land rather than the value of the crop. This often caused widespread distress among peasants because no adjustments were allowed in times of poor harvest. As a result of the land tax the number of tenant farmers increased. Landholdings, meanwhile, became concentrated in the hands of a few wealthy rural families.

Through the introduction of modern farming methods, agricultural production was improved. It became the base which supported Japan's rapid industrialization. In this latter area, the central authorities first sought to develop strategic and heavy industries—communications, munitions, mining, and the merchant marine. At the same time, smaller private enterprise was encouraged and supported with government loans.

Late in the 1870's, foreign technicians were employed and loans obtained from England to build railroads. In the 1880's, the large government-founded heavy industries were sold at low rates to the zaibatsu (see page 10), who were largely drawn from relatives and close friends of the government advisers. This policy marked the beginning of an alliance between government and industry. It was an association which by the 1930's contributed to the failure of parliamentary democracy in Japan. Even today it slows the forces of social reform.

The Meiji Constitution. Meanwhile, a movement in favor of parliamentary government was taking shape. The writer Fukuzawa Yukichi analyzed the political institutions of the United States and England. He concluded that the British parliamentary system was the best form of government. In 1880, Itagaki Taisuke established the *Jiyuto*, or Liberal Party, which was supported by the bulk of the merchants, wealthy peasants, embittered samurai, and enemies of high officials. Although his original purpose was to voice the discontent of the samurai, Itagaki's program became a demand for the election of a popular assembly. As early as 1868, this concept had been given impetus by the emperor's declaration, written by his younger, low-level samurai, of the "Charter Oath." In it he promised that "Deliberative assemblies shall be widely established and all matters decided by public discussion."

The liberal views of Fukuzawa and Itagaki found sympathetic ears with Okuma Shigenobu, a government official who had gained considerable influence over the emperor. Okuma advocated a British-style constitutional monarchy. He was firmly opposed by the conservatives led by Ito, Iwakura, and Yamagata. These and other like-minded officials leaned more toward the Prussian type of constitution in which the emperor would be the sole authority. Although willing to permit the establishment of a cabinet and a parliament, they argued that the emperor should have the right to dissolve either. At the same time, the cabinet should be responsible only to the emperor—its members would not have to be elected parliamentary representatives.

In the contest between the liberals and the conservatives, Ito and Iwakura gradually won the emperor over to their point of view. In October, 1881, Okuma, considered an extremist by other government leaders, was forced to resign. Okuma created a sensation by uncovering an enormous scandal involving the sale of government-owned industries in Hokkaido. In 1882, Okuma formed his own progressive party, the *Kaishinto*, which won considerable support among businessmen and scholars.

To quell the growing popular demand for parliamentary government, the emperor agreed in 1883 that a constitution would be formally drawn up and a parliament called. In the interim, the government would remain in the hands of the conservatives. A select group was delegated the task of writing the constitution, which was to be based on the Prussian model. Ito was sent abroad by the emperor to study foreign constitutions. He and his party spent most of the time in Berlin consulting Prussian constitutional experts, with only a token appearance in London. Returning in 1883, Ito and other officials worked for six years in secret sessions to prepare the document. In the meantime, restrictive laws were passed curtailing the activities of the Progressive and Liberal parties. It was the hope of conservatives that suppression of dissent and a prolonged blackout of news about the constitution would lead to a decline of popular interest in the question.

On February 11, 1889, the emperor handed Ito, the new prime minister, a parchment on which the Japanese Constitution was inscribed. This gesture symbolically conveyed the idea that the Constitution was a gift from the emperor, not the creation of the representatives of the people. Generally speaking, this constitution implemented several basic Japanese ideals: that society is more important than the individual, that men by nature are not equal, that ethics must vary according to political objectives, that government by men is superior to government by law, and that the patriarchal family is the model for the ideal state.

The Japanese Constitution recognized the emperor as all-powerful, sacred, and inviolable. The people, his subjects, were admonished to serve him loyally. Since the constitution was considered a gift of the emperor to his subjects, constitutional amendments could only be made by the emperor himself. To advise the emperor, a privy council was established; it was responsible solely to him. Seven of his most powerful advisers, including conservative leaders of the Satsuma and Choshu clans and Prince Saionji, became known as the *Genro* ("elder statesmen"). Despite the declarations of parliamentary law, these men and their successors were to rule Japan for almost forty years.

A cabinet headed by the prime minister constituted the executive branch of government. Its powers were broad. The cabinet was responsible only to the emperor and not to the lower house of the parliament, as in Western democracies. The military members of the cabinet answered to the emperor alone. He was, in effect, the "commander-in-chief." Yet, unlike his counterparts in Western democracies, he was not subject to recall. The Japanese Parliament, called the *Diet*, was bicameral. The upper house, called the House of Peers, was composed of former daimyo and samurai, members of the nobility, and those who paid large taxes. The lower house, or House of Representatives, was far from representing the whole population. It was voted into office by less than one per cent of the population—those males over twenty-five years of age who paid an annual tax of fifteen yen or more. The upper house shared equal powers with the elected lower house, thus insuring the continuation of conservative policies. In addition, the cabinet had the power to dissolve the Diet at any time. Thus the constitution perpetuated a social structure in which the state was supreme.

The most serious flaw in Japan's system of constitutional government was the complete disregard of the principle of cabinet responsibility. Since the emperor appointed the ministers of army and navy, these public servants were not responsible to their fellow cabinet officials. Neither they nor any party could be held to account for their decisions; they were shielded by the inviolable symbol of the emperor. The arrangement resulted in a kind of dual diplomacy, one pursued by the civilian cabinet members, the other followed by

The Meiji Emperor
(1852–1912)

ministers of the military branches. Thereby the military was able to formulate and carry out policies of which the civilian cabinet officials had no knowledge. While the Meiji leaders were busy adopting Western methods in industrial, technological, and military matters, Western democratic ideals were often totally ignored.

The Constitution had created an electorate of about 450,000, all of whom were males able to pay a tax. Yet it did not give the voters any substantial power because the pro-constitution rulers had learned how to work within the new political process. Prime Minister Ito's predecessor, Yamagata Aritomo, had tried to free himself from popular control by suppressing public meetings and other democratic procedures. The Diet remained an obstacle to him. In contrast, Ito derived parliamentary support by leading in the organization of a new political party. This party, a coalition of the conservatives and "Liberals," was called the Seiyukai. In 1900, it succeeded in gaining Ito his fourth term as prime minister. Unlike his more heavy-handed predecessor, Ito won over his opposition in the Diet by giving them more responsibility rather than by suppressing them. After he resigned in 1901, the militarists were in firm control of the office of prime minister.

Education, religion, and law. The Meiji reform ministers grasped the importance of education; they knew that it would be impossible to create a modern state with an illiterate population. In 1872, Japan instituted compulsory education: all boys and girls had to receive at least six years of schooling. Higher education was also made available for the male population in a number of government-built academies and colleges. Tokyo Imperial University, the most famous, was founded in 1873. A Ministry of Education was created to administer the entire system.

The government received assistance from American educators who went to Japan to help train teachers. However, the Japanese did not embrace American educational values, which stressed individualism. Japan's conservative rulers realized the powerful tool education afforded for molding the minds of the young. Children were inculcated with values of loyalty, service, and obedience to their superiors. Ethics courses, or *shushin*, bulked large in the curriculum. These tendencies were apparent in the Imperial Rescript on education issued in 1890.

. . .be filial to your parents, affectionate to your brothers and sisters; as husbands and wives be harmonious, as friends, true; bear yourselves in modesty and moderation; extend your benevolence to all; pursue learning and cultivate arts, and thereby develop intellectual faculties and perfect moral powers; furthermore, advance public good and promote common interests; always respect the Constitution and observe the laws; should emergency arise, offer yourselves courageously to the State; and thus guard and maintain the prosperity of Our Imperial Throne coeval with heaven and earth. So shall ye not only be Our good and faithful subjects, but render illustrious the best traditions of your forefathers. . . .

The principles expressed by the Imperial Rescript were not shared by every faction in Japan. A group led by Fukuzawa Yukichi urged an educational process that would create an independent-minded populace. Throughout the Meiji era, he and a few colleagues wrote and spoke in behalf of a freer Japanese people. They published many articles, imported Western books, and opened a private university. But they could not overcome the tendency of Japanese educators to value patriotism above independent thought.

The system of education was supplemented by the revival of Shinto, which became the official religion of the state. Shinto helped to instill in the children of Japan feelings of loyalty to the emperor and a keen sense of patriotism. A special bureau of Shinto was created in the government. The practice of Buddhism was simultaneously discouraged. Partly due to the urgings of Western powers, Christianity was made legal in 1873.

The Japanese leaders then began work on a code of law. Their problem was to prepare a code which would incorporate the best elements of Western legal systems and at the same time keep the individual subservient to the state. Once again the Japanese sent missions abroad and invited foreign jurists to help them set up the necessary lawmaking machinery. At length a new criminal code, written along the lines of France's Napoleonic Code, was adopted. For the civil and commercial codes, German models were used. Compromises between traditional Japanese and modern Western legal values were frequently made. For example, all members of a household were still legally under the authority of the father. Yet the wife and children won rights to their own property. Women gained rights but were still at a legal disadvantage in such matters as marriage, divorce, and inheritance. All in all, the Meiji legal reforms were like the educational reforms which stressed the individual's duties, rather than rights, in the state.

Meiji literature. The beginning of the Meiji Restoration was not accompanied by notable changes in the arts. Most Japanese writing continued to draw moral lessons in the traditional way. By the late 1880's, however, Western literature was in great demand. At that time the first successful Japanese novel, *Drifting Cloud*, by Futabatei Shimei, was published. It opened the way to writing in the vernacular and to the development of character in fiction. By the turn of the century, Japan was producing a large number of novels. Reflecting the controversy of the nation itself, they were divided over the issue of whether Japan should accept Western ways or further cultivate its own national traditions.

In 1884 the Japanese government began to administrate more than 80,000 Shinto shrines such as this one in an effort to promote national unity.

JAPAN AS A WORLD POWER: FOREIGN EXPANSION (1894–1918)

By 1894, Japan had undergone spectacular changes: the government had been centralized, a constitution drawn up, an army created, a system of education put into practice, a modern legal code adopted, and a formidable military and industrial machine assembled. In the 1890's, the nation began to make its new power felt in the world. In 1894, Britain agreed to give up its special privileges of extraterritoriality. In 1899, the other Western powers were obliged to follow suit. Japan was in an expansionist mood, determined to prove its right to an equal place among the great powers.

Although the Japanese constitution was firmly established, political discord did not abate. The framers of the Meiji constitution had designed the Diet to serve as a forum with no real power. The Diet struggled to gain authority, however, when the issue of expansionism was revived. Disputes continued between the conservatives who controlled the executive branch and the popular representatives who dominated the lower house of the Diet. The lower house frequently slashed the military budgets requested by such expansionist statesmen as Yamagata. The cabinet, in turn, was split between the military faction under Yamagata's leadership and Ito's civilian group. However, internal political differences were put aside with the outbreak of the Sino-Japanese War.

Sino-Japanese War (1894–1895). For years Japan had been quarreling with China over the status of Korea. In 1885, China and

The Sino-Japanese War (1894–1895) heralded the rise of Japan as a world power. At Heijo (Pyongyang, Korea), the Japanese forces routed the Chinese.

Japan agreed to renounce any claims to exclusive control over the "Hermit Kingdom." Nevertheless, China insisted on the right to conduct Korea's foreign affairs. Chinese influence on the Korean Peninsula increased, to the alarm of Japan's rulers.

In 1894, a rebellion of Korean nationalists provided the excuse for Ito's government to act. Since Chinese troops were entering Korea at the Korean king's invitation to put down the revolt, Japan decided to send her troops uninvited. In July, 1894, Japan and China went to war. By November of that year the well-trained Japanese soldiers, equipped with modern weapons, had routed the Chinese and gained control of all Korea, as well as the Liaotung Peninsula in China. China capitulated and signed a peace treaty at Shimonoseki. Korea was recognized as independent (though in fact Japanese influence there was to increase). Japan took Taiwan (for which it was to use the Portuguese name "Formosa," meaning "beautiful"), the Pescadore Islands, and the Liaotung Peninsula from China. As a final humiliation, China was forced to pay a large indemnity which amply covered Japan's costs in the war.

Taking the West by surprise, Japan had proved that her expanding economy could be turned to conquest. Shortly afterwards, some Western powers, led by Russia, attempted to limit Japanese ambitions. Soon after the conclusion of the peace treaty, Russia, together with France and Germany, insisted that the Liaotung Peninsula be returned to China. Japan was forced to yield, but the Japanese reaction against this "Triple Intervention" was bitter. Patriotic pride was further incensed when Russia later, in 1898, grabbed the Liaotung Peninsula herself. The Japanese concluded that only military might would force the West to treat them as equals. Aggressive nationalism, rather than conciliation and cooperation, seemed to induce respect from the other powers. Not only Japan, but the United States and Great Britain, too, began to wonder how the Russian drive towards the Pacific could be halted.

Russo-Japanese War (1904-1905). In 1902, Japan signed a treaty of alliance with Great Britain. It recognized Britain's special interests in China, and Japan's in Korea. In addition, the two countries acknowledged each other's rights to intervene militarily when and where their interests were endangered. The agreement provided that if one nation became involved in a war to safeguard its rights, the other would remain neutral. The psychological effects of the alliance were far-reaching in Japan. It signaled that Japan had become an equal in the eyes of the West. With Britain on its side, Japan adopted a more belligerent attitude toward Russia, which was challenging Japanese influence in Korea. The emperor's government sought recognition from Russia of its preeminence in Korea, but this the tsarist government was not willing to grant. Negotiations broke

Japan won a stunning victory in her war with Russia (1905). Here, under a white flag of truce, Japanese and Russian officers confer on a battlefield.

down, and Japan prepared for war. The emperor, the government, and the people were confident that their country would emerge victorious.

Hostilities commenced in 1904. To the amazement of Western observers, the Japanese army crushed the tsarist forces in bitter battles near Mukden (capital of Manchuria) and Port Arthur. At the Battle of Tsushima Strait, the Japanese navy under Admiral Togo won an even more stunning victory, brilliantly outmaneuvering and destroying the Russian Baltic fleet which had sailed halfway around the world to take part in the action. Defeated on land and sea, racked by civil strife at home, Russia sought a settlement. At the same time, sizable military losses and financial strains prompted the Japanese government to make peace. President Theodore Roosevelt offered his good offices as a negotiator. At this time, the United States was seeking to strengthen its position in the Philippines. In the so-called Taft-Katsura Agreement, the United States recognized Japan's "Suzereignty over Korea"; Japan, in return, gave assurances of no aggressive designs upon the Philippines. Thus, Japan had the indirect support of the United States at the treaty talks.

In August, 1905, the Treaty of Portsmouth between Russia and Japan was signed. Russia recognized Japan's interests in Korea, while Manchuria was turned over to China. Russia's possessions in the Liaotung Peninsula (including Port Arthur, Darien, and the South Manchurian Railroad) were ceded to Japan. Finally, Japan took over from Russia the southern half of Sakhalin Island. Thus Russian influence in Asia diminished. Japan, moving into Russian positions, began to compete with other Western powers with investments there.

Seizure of Korea (1910). Although Russia recognized Japanese influence in Korea, the Koreans themselves were never consulted.

The Koreans were reluctant to submit to this kind of power diplomacy. The Korean kingdom secretly sought aid from the United States, but President Theodore Roosevelt closed the American Legation in Seoul and acknowledged Korea as a Japanese protectorate.

Japan sent Prince Ito to Korea as its first resident general. Ito took control of Korea's foreign affairs, then imposed a series of domestic "reforms" covering agriculture, transportation, and reorganization of the courts and police forces—all beneficial to the Japanese. By 1907, the Japanese resident general had assumed the right to approve the appointment of high Korean officials. Ito found the Koreans difficult to deal with. They remained strongly devoted to self-rule and were deeply resentful of the presence of the Japanese. Although Ito's policies were accepted by the Korean government, the stubborn officials blocked them. Korean protests were harshly repressed. In Japan militant groups, such as the Amur River Society, demanded outright annexation so that the Koreans could be more effectively controlled.

In 1909, Ito was replaced as resident general by General Terauchi Masatake. A year later Ito, while on an inspection tour of Manchuria, was assassinated by a fanatical Korean nationalist. In July, 1910, General Terauchi retaliated by bringing troops into Korea and placing the country under martial law. In August of the same year, the Korean government capitulated. A treaty was signed whereby Japan annexed Korea, and the country was placed under Japanese law. The administration of Korea was left in the hands of the Japanese military, who strove ruthlessly to eradicate Korean nationalist feelings. Yet, at the end of World War II, the Koreans still kept alive a keen patriotism and a violent hatred against Japan.

World War I and the Twenty-One Demands. When World War I erupted in Europe, the Japanese realized that by the terms of the Anglo-Japanese alliance they were expected to render some form of aid to the Allied cause. Foreign Minister Kato Komei considered the hostilities in Europe ideal for Japan's national interests. Principally, it offered an opportunity to root out German bases in China and certain Pacific islands and to extend Japanese power into those areas.

In 1914, the Japanese government ordered Germany to surrender its possessions in the Chinese Shantung Peninsula. Receiving no response from the Kaiser's government, Japan declared war and dispatched troops to Shantung. There the Germans surrendered after only token resistance. Japanese naval forces then moved on to the German-controlled islands in the Pacific: the Marianas, the Carolines, and the Marshalls. Small German contingents on the Islands also surrendered without trouble. This was Japan's only real contribution to the allied war effort. It was given at little cost, for great gain.

Since the Western powers were embroiled in Europe, Foreign Minister Kato decided that the time was appropriate to move against a weak, decentralized China. In May, 1915, Japan submitted her notorious Twenty-One Demands to President Yuan Shih-kai of China. These demands, rendered as ultimatums, were in five groups. The first four groups demanded for Japan the German bases in Shantung Province, economic concessions in Manchuria and Inner Mongolia, and other preferential trading rights. The demands of the fifth group were the most arrogant and, if accepted by China, would have made her a Japanese protectorate. Under them, Japanese officials would have joined the Chinese government as "advisers." Militarily weak, China gave in to the first four groups of demands, but was able to forestall action on the fifth.

During 1917, Japan reached secret understandings with Britain, the United States, France, and Italy on the Chinese question. Britain was willing to honor Japan's claims to the Shantung Peninsula in return for Japanese recognition of Britain's future control of German islands south of the equator. In the Lansing-Ishii Agreement, the United States acknowledged Japan's special interest in China in those areas contingent to Japanese possessions. In return, Japan agreed not to interfere with the United States economic concessions in China. The other Allied powers were willing to grant the Japanese their demands if they would persuade China to break relations with Germany. The Japanese envoy Nishihara was able to convince the corrupt warlords of Peking to declare war on Germany by promises of loans. He also extended Japan's influence on the mainland by making loans to the central government there.

When the Russian Revolution broke out in 1917, Japan ordered warships to the port of Vladivostok in Siberia to prevent the Bolsheviks from seizing supplies which the Allies had stored there. In 1918, a large Allied expeditionary force landed in Siberia to fight the Bolsheviks. Later, with the approval of the Allies, Japan also dispatched military forces to Siberia, for the same reason. Although small numbers of Allied troops were stationed in Vladivostok, Eastern Siberia was controlled by the Japanese army.

Japan at the Versailles Peace Conference. Japan went to Versailles eager to have its secret agreements with the Allies fulfilled. The Japanese were also caught up in the emotionalism of President Wilson's liberal program for the peace settlement. They believed a new era in international relations had dawned in which the principle of racial equality would be accepted in practice. The Japanese had grown extremely sensitive to the racial intolerance of such countries as the United States, which discriminated against Asians. The Japanese hoped that a clause repudiating racial discrimination would be inserted in the League of Nations Covenant.

At Versailles, the racial question proved difficult for Great Britain because of the hostile attitude of Australia toward immigration of Asians. The United States delegation supported the principle of racial equality because the Japanese privately agreed not to complicate matters by bringing up the immigration problem. However, pressure from racist groups at home embarrassed the American delegation. When Britain decided to side with Australia, the equality clause was not inserted in the Covenant to the League of Nations.

Smarting from the insult, the Japanese determined not to yield their conquests in the Shantung Peninsula. Japanese ambitions suffered a temporary setback when the United States showed sympathies with Chinese demands for the return to China of the former German holdings in Shantung. But Britain did hold to its secret agreement and supported the Japanese claims.

On its official level China ratified these claims, but the Chinese people angrily rejected them. Several thousand students, educators, and politicians gathered in Peking to begin what became known as the "May 4th Movement"—an alliance of intellectuals and merchants who were determined to uproot Japanese influence in their country. Although it firmly suppressed anti-Japanese strikes and boycotts, the Chinese government was forced to oppose Japan's claim to the Shantung Peninsula. President Wilson, while aware of the moral rightness of China's position, understood the need for Britain's support in a future League of Nations. Italy had already walked out of the Versailles Conference, and Japan threatened to do likewise. Finally, Wilson agreed to allow Japan to keep the former German concessions in China. The Chinese, highly indignant, refused to sign the Versailles treaty.

Thus Japan, though rebuffed on the racial question, obtained all her other demands. She took over the German leases in Shantung and (as controlled "mandates" for the League of Nations) the former German islands in the Pacific which she had seized during the war.

Chapter 7

JAPAN BETWEEN THE TWO WORLD WARS

WHILE THE JAPANESE ENVOYS were winning diplomatic victories at Versailles, the country was experiencing severe domestic stresses and strains. The central problem was the phenomenal population increase. With the introduction of modern scientific and medical techniques, the population skyrocketed between 1860 and 1920 from thirty-five million to fifty-five million. Demand for all products increased, raising prices and reducing supplies to a dangerous level. After 1910, the nation was forced to import food from abroad. At the end of World War I food shortages led to riots throughout Japan.

Although Japan's industrial development had been highly successful, emphasis was upon the production of capital goods and war equipment. She had been a supplier of goods to the Allies during World War I and had intensively developed markets in Asia. However, consumer goods were scarce and the living standards of the people remained low. Urban population increased rapidly as peasants left their farm to seek work in the new steel plants and textile mills. Work days were long and wages low. After the disastrous Tokyo-Yokohama earthquake of September, 1923, a great modern city was built on the ruins—a symbol of the new era. Meanwhile, the rural population shrank proportionally, and hard times set in on the Japanese farms. Food prices fell after the war, and poverty on farms became widespread. In the 1920's, many farmers turned to silkworm production to supplement their income.

In time the growing industrial work force formed labor unions and demanded better wages, working conditions, and a voice in the political process. The dissident rural population also began to organize. Many farmers, having lost their land because of wide market fluctuations, protested what seemed to be a lack of official concern for their welfare. But neither the workers nor the farmers posed a serious threat to the conservative government. The unions represented less than ten per cent of the work force. Neither the Socialist nor the Communist party gained much popular support. The government, with the financial aid of the zaibatsu, controlled dissidence by means of censorship and police action.

SUCCESSES AND FAILURE OF PARLIAMENTARY GOVERNMENT
(1918–1931)

As the Meiji leaders died, cracks appeared in the once-solid oligarchy that dominated Japan. There were conflicts between the bureaucracy, the military, and the political parties that had been arising. Subordinate to the Meiji emperor until his death in 1912, they became increasingly outspoken, although far from representative of their constituency, under the rule of the Taisho emperor.

In 1918, for the first time since the promulgation of the Japanese Constitution, a commoner, Hara Kei, was asked to establish a cabinet. Hara, whose Seiyukai Party (originally formed by Prince Ito and his followers) dominated the lower house of the Diet, appointed cabinet members from his party—with the important exception of the ministers of army and navy, who were still appointed by the emperor from the highest ranks of the military.

Premier Hara was a talented politician who deftly manipulated the contending forces inside of Japan. He built up the strength of his party with the support of small rural landlords, in part by reducing the financial restrictions on voters. Yet, at a time when he might have expanded democratic participation in government he chose not to allow universal manhood suffrage. Sacrificing his promised reforms to his hopes for economic development, he introduced measures to crush unions, using tactics similar to those of the old Meiji leaders. Unfortunately for the infant Japanese labor unions, their activities were confused by many with the programs of the Marxists—and thus resisted all the more fiercely by the middle and upper classes.

Committed to a policy of increasing Japan's influence in China, Hara extended the country's dependence upon the military at a time when it was threatening to take control of the government. Student riots and strikes plagued his administration and continued through 1921, when he was assassinated. With his death, the conservative Seiyukai Party disintegrated, and in June, 1922, the control of the government reverted to non-party cabinets. The first attempt at true parliamentary government had failed.

The Washington Conference (1921–1922). Perhaps Japan's entrance into the League of Nations in 1920 signalled a new era—one of international cooperation. The Washington Conference was convened not long afterwards to deal with the China question with the hopes of assuring that peaceful cooperation would continue. Frustrated by her inability to oppose Japanese demands at Versailles and alarmed over the increasing influence of Japan in the Far East, the United States invited the world's major powers to a disarmament conference. The participants concluded a number of important treaties.

By participating in the conference, Japan was able to forestall a potential race with the United States. However, the seemingly moderate policies pursued by party leaders in their treaty negotiations met with increasingly bitter debate from the military. Japan's professional soldiers did not want any limitation on their right to increase the country's relative strength.

Although the Washington Conference achieved part of its goal in establishing a program of naval disarmament, it left out much on which the Japanese later capitalized. Nothing was said about the size of the army or air force; no restrictions were placed on vessels below the class of battleships such as destroyers and submarines. In those areas, not covered by the conference agreement, Japan busily built up her strength. Yet, not even this seeming diplomatic victory pleased the Japanese military, who thought that any arms limitation was a compromise of their defensive posture.

Conflict between Parliament and the military (1924–1931). By 1924, only Prince Saionji, a proponent of parliamentary government, was left of the old Meiji government's Genro clique; all others had died. After a series of crises, the cabinet was again turned over to a party leader, this time to Kato Komei. He led the coalition Kenseikai group which supported party control of government, curtailment of the military, civilian control over all national affairs, and party-dominated cabinets. Under his leadership, the Diet passed a law extending the franchise to all males twenty-five or over (without the tax payment requirement)—an increase of more than 10,000,000 voters. Labor legislation was introduced and social welfare measures enacted. The Imperial Army was reduced in size. Kato's moderate foreign minister, Shidehara Kijuro, concluded a treaty with the Soviet Union in 1925. It recognized the revolutionary government established by the Bolsheviks. Japanese forces were withdrawn from Siberia and northern Sakhalin.

These liberal measures were balanced, however, by reactionary moves to insure autocratic control of the government. Stringent

In the 1920's, Japanese militarists persecuted liberals, who are seen here rioting over a repressive law.

"Peace Preservation" laws regulated the activities of the people. A special branch of the police was created to combat "dangerous thought," and long prison terms were given to advocates of constitutional or social changes. Finally, although Kato's government cut back the strength of the Imperial Army, discharged officers were reassigned to teach in schools, where military courses were made compulsory. Militarism steadily penetrated the Japanese school system. Military ministers in the Cabinet needed only the approval of their respective services to gain their posts.

Between 1924 and 1931, Kato, Shidehara, and other supporters of constitutional government tried to control the militarists, who were pressing for overseas expansion. The army opposed any policy of international cooperation. The militarists argued that foreign conquest was the only outlet for Japan's rapidly expanding population, which was outrunning the country's resources. They pointed out that the Western nations, especially the United States, had practically closed their doors to immigrants from Asia. Since 1900, Japanese immigrants had been subjected to special abuse in the state of California. When in 1906 the city of San Francisco sought to exclude Chinese and Japanese from its public schools, President Theodore Roosevelt was obliged to intervene. An agreement was reached whereby Japan consented not to grant passports to emigrating Japanese laborers. In return San Franicisco rescinded its school exclusion laws. Nevertheless, resentment lingered. As we saw, it was again inflamed by the failure of the Western nations to include a racial equality clause in the League of Nations Covenant.

In 1924, the United States passed a harsher immigration law which virtually barred Asian immigrants. (Australia and New Zealand excluded them entirely.) The Japanese militarists seized upon the exclusion clause of the United States Immigration Law as a justification for their expansionist policies.

Premier Kato died in 1927. He was replaced by a militarist, General Tanaka. His cabinet was alarmed over the growing strength

General Tanaka, leader
of the militarists,
became premier in 1927
and toasted the victory of
the war party.

of Chiang Kai-shek, who was slowly bringing all China under his control. By 1928, most of the Western countries had recognized Chiang's regime and given up many of their special privileges obtained from the inept Manchus during the nineteenth century. The Chinese had also begun boycotting Japanese goods. When Chiang's armies moved northward from his headquarters in South China, the Japanese feared for their holdings in Shantung and Manchuria. Kato's government had exercised restraint in not intervening against Chiang's northern expedition (1926-1927). But in 1928, General Tanaka, without informing the Diet, dispatched troops to Shantung. China was forced to yield to Japan's ultimatum demanding an end to the boycott of Japanese goods.

The officers of the Japanese armies garrisoning the Liaotung (or Kwantung) Peninsula and guarding the South Manchurian Railroad were among those most ambitious to further their country's interests on the Asian mainland. These military men were anxious to strengthen Japan's position in Manchuria, where the Chinese warlord Chang Tso-lin was becoming difficult to control. These officers were prepared to use terrorist tactics. With the arrival of Japanese troops in Shantung, they initiated a series of events which culminated in the bombing of a train carrying Chang Tso-lin in 1928. Evidence clearly showed that officers of the Japanese "Kwantung Army" were responsible for the incident.

The insubordination of the Japanese army in Manchuria and the government's failure to punish those responsible for the murder of Chang Tso-lin forced Tanaka's resignation. His government was replaced by that of a moderate, Hamaguchi Osachi. In this administration, Shidehara Kijuro, Kato's liberal foreign minister, returned to his old place. Hamaguchi sought to curtail military expenditures and adopted a more conciliatory policy toward China. But the efforts of Hamaguchi and other supporters of party government to restrain the military were frustrated by the pressures of world events.

THE TRIUMPH OF THE MILITARY (1931-1937)

The World Depression, which began in 1929, greatly strengthened the position of the militarists. Since Japan was almost entirely dependent upon foreign trade, the effects of the collapse of the world market were devastating. The loss, for example, of the American market for silks ruined the thousands of Japanese farmers who in the 1920's had taken up silkworm-raising.

By 1925, most of Japan's small industries had been replaced or totally crushed by the giant monopolies of the zaibatsu, who had a stranglehold on the finances of the country. With wealth concentrated in the hands of the zaibatsu, no large liberal middle class was left to oppose the militarists. The peasants were deeply in debt. The Depression threw millions of industrial laborers out of work and reduced them to a level of bare subsistence. In addition, Japanese students were keenly discontented because they saw no chances for advancement in a government controlled by politicians and financial cliques.

Militaristic sentiment was fanned by thousands of junior army officers from rural areas. These men formed the backbone of the Kwantung Army. Harking back to the swashbuckling days of the samurai, they distrusted professional politicians, who were suspected of making shady deals and selling out the country to the big business interests. They blamed the politicians and the zaibatsu for the disastrous Depression.

Service in Manchuria confirmed the radical views of these officers on foreign affairs. They saw in Japanese conquest of Asia's resources and markets a remedy for the distress caused by the Depression as well as an outlet for the burgeoning population. On the homefront, they began demanding the abrogation of the Constitution, the dissolution of the Diet, and the creation of a government by martial law. They condemned Western ideas as alien to the Japanese spirit and called for the revival of national traditions and patriotism. In many ways, their program was similar to that of the contemporary movements in Nazi Germany and Fascist Italy.

As an organized movement, extreme nationalism in Japan was conceived by Kita Ikki in the 1920's. Kita's book, *An Outline Plan for the Reconstruction of Japan*, proposed a military takeover that would sweep out the officials around the emperor, replacing them with soldiers. He favored the nationalization of industry and the expansion of Japan's activity throughout Asia. During the 1930's, increasing numbers of military men joined anti-capitalist, right-wing societies which espoused this program. Some joined secret societies such as the Cherry Blossom Association and the Amur River Society—seemingly harmless names that were masks for the advocates of aggression.

The militarists were aroused to fury by diplomatic developments in the 1930's. In 1930, a Naval Conference was held in London. At the London Naval Conference, Premier Hamaguchi agreed that the power of the Japanese navy should continue to be restricted. Over the violent protests of the Japanese navy, the privy council accepted the London Naval Treaty which called for a 10:6 ratio between the Western powers and Japan in battleship construction until 1936. The military faction claimed the nation had been betrayed. Terroristic attacks upon liberals and moderates occurred throughout Japan. This campaign of terror led to the shooting of Premier Hamaguchi in November, 1930.

The Manchurian Incident (1931).   While at home the militarists were attempting to terrorize the political party leaders into submission, the Japanese army in Manchuria decided on bolder action. In justification of their plan they cited the growing strength of Chiang's army and the threat posed by Soviet troops along the Amur River. On September 18, 1931, a big explosion occurred outside the city of Mukden near the South Manchurian railroad line. The next morning the citizens of Mukden awoke to find the Japanese army in complete control of the city. Claiming that the explosion had been an attempt by Chinese rebels to bomb a train, the Japanese poured troops into Manchuria. While the Japanese government tried to explain the incident to the League of Nations, the emperor was persuaded to approve the army's action. The civilian government in Tokyo lost all control over the Manchurian army leaders.

In Geneva, the League of Nations debated the Manchurian incident and finally sent a commission, headed by Lord Lytton, to investigate. The League, however, proved unwilling to punish the aggression. Yet in 1933, Japan withdrew from the international organization. Meanwhile, the Japanese army consolidated its control in Manchuria and set up the puppet state of "Manchukuo," headed by Henry Pu-yi, the heir to China's Manchu Dynasty. In the early 1930's, outstanding critics of the army's policies were assassinated. On May 15, 1932, a group of young militarists murdered Premier Inukai. As one weak cabinet succeeded another, the government became increasingly subservient to the army and navy. Later, the Japanese Kwantung Army moved from its bases in Manchuria into the Chinese northern and northwestern provinces. These forces penetrated well beyond the Great Wall of China.

In February, 1936, radical elements in the army carried out a military coup and threw out the cabinet. The most important prominent moderates of the government were murdered. Though the insurrection, led by junior officers, was finally put down, it further weakened the liberal party forces. In 1936, the Japanese signed the Anti-Comintern Pact with Hitler's Germany. The stage was now set for Japan's invasion of the rest of China.

Invasion of China (1937). In 1937, the Japanese demanded of the Chinese government the suppression of anti-Japanese news reports, the right to inspect Chinese schools to remove teachers hostile to Japan, the recognition of a separate political structure in North China, and lastly, a joint expedition against the Chinese Communist rebels, located in northwest China. Chiang Kai-shek refused; negotiations between the two countries broke down.

General Tojo Hideki, the commander of the Japanese Kwantung Army, urged a direct attack upon China. The surviving moderates believed that economic domination of China could be achieved without alienating Britain and the United States by a military invasion. A compromise cabinet was formed by Prince Konoye in

In 1937, the Japanese army overran and destroyed Nanking. Celebrating the triumph, Division Commander Matsui reviewed his troops in the city.

1937. However, Konoye proved unable to resist the demands of the radical military right wing. In July, 1937, a clash took place between Japanese and Chinese troops at the Marco Polo Bridge outside Peking. The Kwantung Army called for, and received large reinforcements. Later in the month, full-scale war broke out between Japan and China.

The Japanese next turned their attention to the south and seized Shanghai. They then moved up the Yangtze River Valley toward the capital, Nanking. The United States attempted to arrange a peaceful settlement. Konoye's government offered to negotiate, provided the United States and other Western powers recognized Japan's special interests in China. But Chiang refused to acknowledge Japan's superiority on the Asian continent. The conciliation effort came to nothing, and despite valiant Chinese resistance, the Japanese advanced further into the interior. Nanking fell; it was looted and devastated.

Still, by 1938, the Japanese militarists had discovered that the Chinese could not easily be subdued. The military leaders sought to mobilize the entire Japanese nation for the war effort. All urban households became members of neighborhood councils. A National Mobilization Law was passed which abolished the remaining civil liberties. The law introduced radio and press censorship, government control of wages, prices, and production, and wartime taxes. In addition, key governmental posts were turned over directly to military officers. By 1940, the last vestiges of parliamentary government had disappeared. As a substitute for political parties, a super-nationalistic body called the "Imperial Rule Assistance Association" was formed. It was made up of the military, members of the Diet, business interests, and patriotic organizations. Ultimately nearly all other organizations in the country joined the association, which was regulated in order to "maximize assistance to the emperor."

Manchuria and the Japanese-controlled regions of North China were politically and economically integrated with the home islands to benefit the war machine. Grandiose plans were made by the Japanese government. They called for a "Greater East Asia Co-Prosperity Sphere." Through it, conquered Asian countries would supply raw materials to and furnish markets for state-regulated Japanese industry. The great economic combines, however, resisted efforts to place their enterprises under absolute government control. The zaibatsu did not oppose the control of wages, but objected to government regulation of prices. It was not until September, 1941, that a compromise was reached between the powerful zaibatsu interests and the military. With the formation of the enormous industrial-military complex, the zaibatsu agreed to supply the needs of the war economy. They never gave away full control of their companies, however.

The Road to Total War

In the 1930's, Japanese relations with the Soviet Union had steadily deteriorated. The Soviet Union had signed a non-aggression pact with China in 1937. In 1938 and 1939, clashes occurred along the Manchurian border between Japanese and Russian troops. But after the signing of the non-aggression pact between Russia and Germany in 1939, Japan's relations with the Soviet Union improved. In 1940, Japan joined Germany and Italy in a tripartite alliance. The so-called Axis Pact recognized the leadership of Germany and Italy in Europe and of Japan in "Greater East Asia." All three agreed to help each other in case of an attack from an outside power (such as the United States). A prime aim of the pact was to discourage the United States from efforts to halt Japanese advancement in Asia.

By 1939, Japan felt free to increase its pressure on the Western powers. Taking advantage of the strong isolationist sentiment in the United States, the Japanese began to squeeze out foreign competitors in China. The United States, unwilling to risk war, limited itself to diplomatic protests. In 1939 and 1940, Japan tried to sever Western aid to Chiang Kai-shek. They cut the principal lifeline to China, the British-built road across Burma. They also occupied the northern region of French Indochina and the French-controlled island of Hainan in the South China Sea. Menaced by Hitler in Europe, France and Great Britain could do nothing. France fell to the Nazi war machine in June, 1940. Britain was fighting for its life.

The Japanese were quick to take advantage of Britain's plight. They blockaded foreign concessions in Tientsin and searched all people leaving the city, hoping to find the British smuggling silver out of China. The Chinese had given the British the silver as collateral for loans. Western women were humiliated by having to strip in public to show that they were not hiding anything. By this practice, Japan sought to deflate the prestige of the West in China. It also showed the Chinese that Japan was the self-appointed deliverer of Asia from the colonial powers. But Britain refused to give up the Chinese silver to Japan. The United States reacted by terminating the important Treaty of Commerce with Japan. It had been in existence since 1911. The United States warned Japan that if she did not cease abusing American subjects, who were among those searched, an embargo would be imposed. This was something which Japan could not afford at this time.

Hitler's invasion of the Soviet Union in June, 1941, caught the Japanese by surprise. Torn between a recent non-aggression pact with Russia (concluded in April, 1941) and the Axis treaty with Germany, Foreign Minister Matsuoka advocated declaring war on Russia. This plan was rejected, however, and the Japanese merely promised Hitler to enter the war "later." Meanwhile, the Japanese militarists decided the time was right for an aggressive move in Southeast Asia. In July, 1941, the Japanese, in cooperation with Vichy French colonial forces, occupied south Indochina and Siam (later called Thailand).

The United States retaliated by freezing Japanese assets in America and imposing an embargo on oil shipments to Japan. The Japanese war machine was dependent upon imports of oil. The militarists in Japan faced two alternatives: they could withdraw from Indochina, or they could assure their oil supply by seizing the rich oil fields in the Dutch East Indies. The latter move was sure to mean war not only with Holland but also with the United States.

Prince Fumimaro Konoye
(1891–1945), unable to resist
the military while serving as
Japan's premier, proclaimed
"a new order in Asia."

After a temporary rupture in Japanese-American negotiations, Prince Konoye's militarist-dominated government decided that contacts should be resumed. He sought the means to persuade the United States to accept Japan's occupation of Indochina. Konoye proposed a top-level meeting between himself and President Roosevelt. Cordell Hull, the American Secretary of State, insisted that Japanese troops had to be withdrawn before a meeting of the heads of state could take place. The Japanese military was resolved to fight rather than retreat. In October, Prince Konoye resigned, unable to reconcile military and civilian interests. He was replaced as premier by General Tojo Hideki, a step that resulted in a military dictatorship.

Tojo set November 29 as a deadline for negotiations with the United States: if they failed, Japan would go to war. The last diplomatic note from the United States reached Japan on November 26 and was rejected. Carefully prepared war plans were now put into action by Tojo's government. While Japan's final note of reply was being deciphered at the Japanese Embassy in Washington, D.C., Japanese naval forces moved toward Pearl Harbor, the great American naval base in Hawaii.

After attacking Pearl Harbor the Japanese moved quickly to take over French, British, and Dutch colonies in Asia. This scene is in Malaya.

CHAPTER 8

WAR, DEFEAT, AND REHABILITATION

ON SUNDAY, DECEMBER 7, 1941, while in Washington efforts were still being made to reopen negotiations, the Japanese carried out a surprise attack on the large United States naval base at Pearl Harbor in Hawaii. Caught unprepared, the United States lost more than 90 percent of its Pacific-based naval and air strength in two hours. While this raid was in progress, Japanese land, naval, and air forces also launched attacks on the Philippines, Malaya, Guam, Wake, and Midway islands, as well as Hong Kong and Singapore.

For the next six months, the American and British forces could do little to hold back the Japanese advance. Manila fell on January 2, 1941 (although the fortress of Corregidor lasted out a long siege until May 6). Singapore was captured on February 15, and in March the Japanese overran the Dutch East Indies and Burma, cutting off the famous Burma Road, a supply route in China. The Solomons, the Gilberts, and other vital South Pacific islands were also seized. Part of the enormous success of the Japanese forces can be traced to the long-standing isolationist policy in the United States and to the Washington Conference in 1922 in which the United States and Britain agreed to limit fortifications and naval bases in the Pacific. The Japanese war machine had been brought to a peak of efficiency. It rolled swiftly and relentlessly over the under-garrisoned and poorly-supplied Western Pacific outposts.

By the middle of 1942, Tojo and his war cabinet had attained several major objectives. The Western colonial powers had been expelled from Southeast Asia. A perimeter of defense had been created around Japan, with Singapore, Manila, and Hong Kong as the strategic bases. The Japanese also had won rich territories with enough mineral resources and croplands to sustain a "Greater East Asia Co-Prosperity Sphere." In addition, millions of Asians regarded Japan at this time as a liberator of colonial nations. Nevertheless, military control of the conquered regions had to continue until friendly native governments could be established. On the Asian mainland the conflict with China still dragged on. Finally, the United States was far from beaten and was determined never to accept the Japanese conquests. Though reeling from the blow against Pearl Harbor, America began mobilizing her industrial might and

During World War II, militarism was widespread in Japan. Even young children dressed up in uniforms and waved flags at the parades.

girding herself for a great effort to repel the aggressors.

Japan soon would feel the effect of its own miscalculations. Unlike the Allied forces, the Japanese failed to coordinate their plans carefully with the other Axis powers. Nor did they build up their air power, which had been so important in the early stages of the war. Perhaps most important, the Japanese military leaders were not united in a course of action.

The Japanese offensive wave was at last halted in May and June of 1942 when the revived United States Navy scored decisive victories at the battles of the Coral Sea and Midway. The Coral Sea engagement thwarted the Japanese plan for expansion further into southeast Pacific waters. At the Battle of Midway (June 4–6, 1942) most of Japan's aircraft carrier forces were destroyed. This was a stunning setback for Japanese military ambitions and prevented further advances eastward to the Hawaiian Islands.

Japan's victories early in the war enhanced the power and prestige of Tojo and his advisers. Tojo placed the conquered Asian countries under harsh military rule. In these countries the Japanese later attempted to set up native collaborationist governments—so that the Japanese could appear to the Asians as "liberators." In 1943, for example, Burma was turned over to a collaborationist regime that helped the Japanese to fight loyal Burmese. In the oil-rich regions of the Dutch East Indies, however, the Japanese military maintained tight control. Japanese officers also continued to govern the Philippines. There the native population refused to cooperate with them and organized guerrilla resistance. As elsewhere in Southeast

Asia, many of the Filipino guerrillas were organized by Communist leaders, a fact that was to produce grave difficulties after the war was over.

In February, 1943, American forces scored an important victory at the Battle of Guadalcanal in the Solomon Islands. By the end of that year, the tide had turned. The United States was threatening the southeastern rim of Japan's defense perimeter. In June, 1944, U.S. forces took Saipan in the Marianas Islands. This American success brought Allied plans within bombing range of Japan. It resulted in the resignation of General Tojo in July, 1944. The new government, headed by Koiso Kuniaki, attempted to prosecute the war with renewed vigor, though to many in the Japanese government it was clear that prospects for victory were slight, the army continued to oppose any kind of compromise peace.

But one Japanese military reverse followed another. Japan was increasingly isolated as the Allies decimated her merchant marine. After the capture of Okinawa by U.S. forces in 1945, massive "saturation" raids were carried out. Terrible "fire raids" destroyed whole sections of major cities. At Leyte Gulf, near the Philippines, one of the greatest naval battles of history was fought. Soon the whole Japanese navy was destroyed. Koiso's government fell. It was replaced by a cabinet headed by Admiral Suzuki Kantaro. Suzuki, a moderate, saw the futility of carrying on the struggle. In April, 1945, an important conference was held with the emperor. Tojo and the army group called for a greater war effort. But Suzuki's cabinet wished to sue for peace.

Allied Policies on Japan: Unconditional Surrender

Two years earlier, in December, 1943, the leaders of Great Britain, the United States, and China had met in Cairo, Egypt. Here, in the Cairo Declaration, the nations most immediately affected by the war in Asia agreed. They agreed furthermore that Japan was to be stripped of all islands seized by her since World War I, that all former Chinese territory was to be returned, and that after Japan's defeat, Korea was in due time to be given her independence. The Allied leaders concluded the conference with a reaffirmation of the announcement (made earlier in the year at the Casablanca Conference between Roosevelt and Churchill) calling for the "unconditional surrender of the Axis states." Later, at the Yalta Conference in February, 1945, efforts were made by the Allies to bring Russia into the war against Japan. Joseph Stalin promised President Franklin D. Roosevelt of the United States and Prime Minister Winston Churchill of Great Britain that the Soviet Union would join the fight against Japan not later than three months after the defeat of Nazi Germany. In return, Russia was to receive special concessions in China and possession of the Kuriles and southern Sakhalin Island.

As the war drew to a close, the Japanese military resolved to make a last stand through the use of suicide pilots, called *Kamikaze* ("divine wind")—the name given to the hurricane that destroyed the invasion fleet of Kublai Khan centuries earlier. Tojo and his group maintained that these tactics would result in such heavy losses for the United States that the Allies would not insist on unconditional surrender. In June, 1945, the emperor consented to allow kamikaze. But two weeks later, he reversed himself. In July, 1945, Emperor Hirohito ordered an envoy sent to Russia (still at peace with Japan) to seek mediation for a settlement with the United States. The only stipulation was that the United States should not insist upon unconditional surrender.

On July 26, 1945, soon after the death of President Roosevelt, President Harry S. Truman issued the Potsdam Declaration, calling on Japan to surrender unconditionally or face destruction. The Potsdam Declaration demanded that militarists and nationalists be eliminated from positions of authority, that Japan's war machinery be destroyed, that war criminals be punished. It also specified that Japanese sovereignty should be limited to the four main islands and adjacent small islands. On the positive side, the declaration stated that Japanese troops abroad would be allowed to return home, civil liberties reestablished, and non-military industries permitted to return to production. Ten days were granted for a reply.

There was no response from the Japanese government. After the first ten days had passed, the United States dropped an atomic bomb, the first in history, on Hiroshima. Almost the entire city was destroyed by that one bomb. More than 100,000 Japanese perished. On August 8, to the shock of the Japanese government, the Soviet Union declared war on Japan. Russian armies invaded Manchuria. At the height of the emergency, a six-man Supreme Council of Japan met on August 9, the day after the Soviet invasion. Three council members favored surrender, with the understanding that the position of the emperor be left unchanged; the other three insisted upon conditions. The tie was broken by the emperor. He called for unconditional acceptance of the Potsdam Declaration with the understanding that the imperial institution would remain. On the same day, the United States dropped a second atomic bomb on Nagasaki.

On September 14, 1945, the war against Japan came to an end. A few weeks later, on September 2, 1945, formal surrender ceremonies took place on the United States battleship *Missouri* in Tokyo Bay. The emperor broadcast the news of surrender to the home population, as well as to the troops stationed overseas. The time had come, he said, ". . . to pave the way for a grand peace for all generations to come by enduring the unendurable and suffering what is insufferable." Though a number of fanatical military leaders, feeling humiliated, committed suicide (*harakiri*), the great mass of the population accepted the surrender without protest.

The American Occupation (1945–1951)

Japan was placed under a military government—SCAP (Supreme Command of the Allied Powers). General Douglas MacArthur assumed command of SCAP. Although an Allied commission, representing the United States, Great Britain, the Soviet Union, and China, was set up to formulate policy, MacArthur wielded the real power on the spot in Tokyo and made most of the important decisions. Each branch of the Japanese government was given a counterpart in MacArthur's office.

Emperor Hirohito commanded the people to obey the occupation authorities. The people heeded his will. Their acceptance of his decision enabled SCAP to take over the Japanese government with little difficulty. More than 200,000 officials were removed from their positions, almost all of them military men. At the start of the occupation, the Japanese army was demobilized and the leading militarists, including Tojo, tried and executed. The nation was limited to the home islands, and millions of Japanese were repatriated from overseas. The state cult of Shinto was abolished. In October, 1945, SCAP issued directives which guaranteed the people basic human rights, rescinded the powers of the once-formidable Japanese police force, and released political prisoners.

In 1945, Japanese leaders were tried for war crimes. Here they are being taken to court in a bus, guarded by United States Military Police.

National elections were held in 1946. The franchise was extended to all persons over twenty years of age. For the first time in the history of Japan, women were given the vote. The restoration of political debate led to the formation of new political parties, including the Japanese Communist Party under Nosaka Sanzo. The Japanese "Progressive" and "Liberal" parties (both reflecting conservative points of view) drew the bulk of their strength from the prewar conservative elements of society. The Social Democrats were supported by the labor unions and the intelligentsia. The election of April, 1946, resulted in control of the Diet by the Progressive and Liberal parties. Yoshida Shigeru, head of the Liberal Party, became Japan's first postwar prime minister.

Although SCAP still held ultimate authority, Japan under Yoshida's leadership began to make rapid strides toward democratic self-government. Upon the insistence of SCAP, the Japanese government adopted a new constitution in 1947.

All Japan was stunned by this picture of General MacArthur, seemingly informal, in the presence of Emperor Hirohito.

The new constitution. The Japanese constitution of 1947, prepared under the supervision of SCAP, was a highly liberal document.
It granted new powers to the people. The emperor was stripped
of his arbitrary authority and reduced to a figurehead. He remained a
symbol of Japanese traditions but no longer was above criticism. For
centuries the man who occupied this position had been considered by
all Japanese to be their spiritual father. Under the new constitution,
the emperor was granted power by the people, not the reverse.

The people began to control their government through a
bicameral Diet. The new lower chamber, the House of Representatives, was given greater authority than the upper one, the House of
Councillors.

For the first time in Japan the principle of cabinet responsibility
was introduced. That is, the representatives in the lower chamber
were given the power to check on cabinet members and also to elect
the premier.

Another basic constitutional change was the separation of the
judiciary from the executive branch of the government. A supreme
court was created with full judicial powers. Judges were elected
by the people for terms of ten years. Finally, a "Bill of Rights" was
drawn up which guaranteed the Japanese people basic liberties
similar to those enjoyed by Americans. The right of workers to
organize and bargain collectively was also promised.

One statement inserted in the constitution renounced the use of
force to settle international disputes. However, the Japanese were
permitted to maintain a small "self-defense" force which resembled a
national police agency rather than an army. With the deterioration
of American-Soviet relations after the war, the United States did not
oppose the growth of this force. It began to look upon Japan as a
potential ally and became eager to help in its rehabilitation.

At first many Japanese regarded the new constitution as an alien
document—which in fact it was, for it was written by officials of
SCAP. In proclaiming the importance of the individual, it ran
counter to the Japanese concept that personal desires must be
sacrificed to the family or a group resembling it. Moreover, it was
seemingly contradictory for an occupation force to be directing a
conquered people to be free. Yet in a relatively short time the
Japanese were using the new constitution effectively, to their political
and economic advantage.

Economic and social reforms. The occupation authorities at first
encouraged reforms that would limit Japan's war-making powers.
They called for the payment of reparations and for the restriction of
the country's industrial capacity. Soon it became clear that the
reparations demanded were larger than all of the assets of the
economy. Furthermore, in the middle of 1947, Japan was in a serious

economic crisis. The cost of living had skyrocketed, and the foreign trade balance was unfavorable. MacArthur then altered his policy. Primary emphasis was placed on the reconstruction of the country rather than on punishment.

To prevent widespread starvation and disease, SCAP imported large shipments of food and medical supplies from the United States. It also induced the Yoshida government to institute rationing and to impose controls on wages and prices. These measures the conservative government, which was sensitive to the pressure of businessmen, accepted only reluctantly.

The most revolutionary economic reform undertaken during the American occupation was the Land Reform Act of October, 1946. Legislation was passed which required absentee landlords to sell their holdings to the government. Tenants were permitted to buy land by borrowing from the government, repaying in installments and at low interest rates. The land reform program was highly successful. By 1950, three million cultivators had acquired possession of over five million acres of land. This reform was so effective that all attempts by the former absentee landlords to regain the land after the end of the Allied occupation failed.

Significant reforms were also sponsored in labor relations. Workers now enjoyed the constitutional right to strike and to bargain collectively, and Japan witnessed the rise of two major unions: the All-Japan Federation of Labor and the National Congress of Industrial Unions. Japanese unions were permitted by SCAP to be flexible with respect to its policies. For example, when radical organizers took advantage of the new freedoms by calling crippling strikes, the occupation authorities forbade the walkouts. However, unions in general were encouraged. By 1952, more than six million workers were affiliated with them, in contrast to one-half million before the war.

One of the most complex and difficult reforms attempted at the insistence of SCAP was the dissolution of the zaibatsu and the decentralization of Japan's economy. During the occupation many large Japanese holding companies were liquidated, and shares in the largest enterprises were offered for public sale. But this program of decentralization was hampered by heavy Japanese government criticism. The businessmen pointed out that they had often opposed militarism in Japan. Besides, in 1947, American financial interests began to resist the United States policy. They insisted that the speedy rehabilitation of Japan could best be effected by conserving the traditional economic organization. A rapid economic buildup was thought to take precedence over political and social reforms because of the growing threat from Communist China. After the end of the American occupation in 1951, the efforts to destroy the zaibatsu were discontinued. With the removal of the United States occupation forces, Japan's finances lapsed back into the hands of the prewar business cliques.

Another SCAP reform which proved short-lived was the plan to reshape the Japanese police system. In prewar Japan, the police played an important role in supporting the dictatorial military governments. The early SCAP reforms sought to democratize and decentralize the Japanese police force. However, the extent to which police organizations should be reformed has been Japan's most explosive issue.

In the vital field of education, SCAP enforced fundamental changes in administrative structure and curriculum. Japan's educational system was decentralized, extended, and broken down into local units. Military subjects and ethics courses were purged from the curriculum. The values of individualism, equality of opportunity, and academic freedom were emphasized. On January 1, 1946, Emperor Hirohito was compelled to disavow his divinity and to acknowledge the rights of the Japanese people. In line with this

After World War II, Japanese education placed greater emphasis on individual rights and achievements and less on group solidarity.

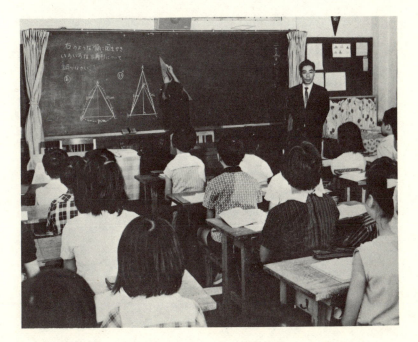

development, chauvinistic history books and other volumes tainted with nationalism or worship of the emperor were replaced by more democratic texts.

The press, including textbooks, was censored during the early phase of the occupation. Later, occupation authorities made freedom of the press one of their major concerns. By the time of their departure, books and news media provided a lively forum for the Japanese people.

Many other reforms were introduced. The Eugenic Protection Act of 1948, which legalized abortions in government clinics under certain circumstances, helped to check the population explosion. It was not introduced or encouraged by the United States, but represented Japan's own attempt to solve a major problem. By 1950, the number of abortions in Japan exceeded live births. All in all, Japan's recovery and rehabilitation were remarkable. In September, 1951, the U.S.-Japanese Peace Treaty was signed in San Francisco and the military occupation ended.

CHAPTER 9

THE ENDURING JAPANESE CULTURE: SOURCE OF NATIONAL PURPOSE

THE FAMILY

DESPITE ITS PASSAGE from feudal into modern times, Japan was inescapably linked to the past through the traditions of its people. Industrialization, warfare, and defeat modified but could not completely change the philosophy on which Japanese life was based. The practice of this philosophy was developed over the centuries and was embedded in the daily activities of the population. In an island country able to preserve its culture in isolation, certain ideas more readily became part of the national character. The one medium through which they were passed from one generation to the next was the family.

The Japanese family was thoroughly organized to perform both as an economic unit and as the source of emotional strength for whoever bore its name. An invisible bond joined its members, living and dead. In evidence of this bond, the head of the traditional family would register all of its members, wherever they lived, in a ledger kept by a local government official. He recorded all changes in the family, including marriages, new households, births, deaths, or adoptions. Thus he proclaimed his responsibility for the members of the family and their responsibility to the tradition which he represented.

In the view of its members, the individuals who made up the family were to be found in all three periods of time: past, present, and future. Their obligation to serve the group well was implied, not only to contemporaries, but also to ancestors and unborn generations. They could identify their family in these ways: first, its nucleus was made up of the eldest males, their wives, and their children in each generation. The younger males and their offspring belonged too, but did not carry the burden of the family tradition as keenly as the eldest. Second, it was an ongoing business which owned property—usually a little land, a house of about twenty by forty feet, and some tools. Third, it had a tradition which was inherent in its occupation and products.

Thus the family was a miniature corporation. It held goods in common and was known widely for whatever it produced. The rest of the community was able instantly to evaluate the family's importance, or social rank.

The family normally included seven or eight persons. The eldest son, his wife, and children would live with his parents, brothers, and sisters. When they married, the family's daughters would move to their husbands' homes. Often a house would become too small for a family. Some of the children would move to one nearby. Nonetheless, the degree of authority in each member of the family would be unchanged. Although a son no longer lived in his father's house, his obligation to obey the father was not diminished, nor was his role in the family altered.

The hierarchical nature of the family. Each member of the family was expected to know his place and neither to rise above nor to fall below it. Age, sex, and the degree of the blood relationship to the head of the family were the determining factors in an individual's position. Older persons were ranked above younger, males above females, and the eldest son above all of his siblings.

At the top stood the father, whose personal loyalty and affection for the first son usually was greater than for other members of the family. The father owed respect to his own parents and grandparents if they were alive, but in Japanese tradition ancestor worship was less pronounced than in China. Esteem for the elderly was applied chiefly to recent generations.

For centuries the Japanese family has given each new generation a strong sense of responsibility. The modern family retains this objective.

Women, particularly the young ones, stood at the bottom of the pyramid. They were thought to be given to the "five weaknesses—disobedience, anger, slanderousness, jealousy, and the lack of intelligence." Prewar Japan granted them few legal rights. They owned no property and without their husbands' approval were unable to buy, sell, borrow, give, or accept possessions. As daughters they were expected to obey their older brothers, father, and mother. As brides they would move into their husbands' homes, where they were often treated as slaves and misfits by their mothers-in-law. As wives they were expected to fulfill their husbands' needs instantly and to refer to them as "Master."

This structure enabled the Japanese family to remain a united, stable social unit, organized to provide economic support and necessary affection over long periods of time. To the average Japanese, life was seen as a constant battle between human emotions (*ninjo*), or the desire to break out of the structure, and moral duties (*on*), or the obligations which the structure imposed. The family existed to help him suppress his emotions so that he could fulfill his moral duties. Its capacity to teach *on* enabled it and the nation to persist through generations of upheaval and strife. Whatever his

In their social and economic lives the Japanese apply the diligence, sense of order, and loyalty that they are taught in their families.

condition, on a farm, in a factory, or at war, every Japanese knew that he had a place in a family to which he belonged and could return.

The extension of hierarchy. The pyramidal shape of authority in the Japanese family ultimately was applied in other relationships. To his superiors the individual was reverent, obedient, and self-sacrificing. When called upon by certain superiors such as his father or the emperor ("The Nation's Father") he would exhibit courage, frugality, self-discipline, and the ability to endure pain. Superiors of a lesser order were treated with courtesy and respect, special terms for which were developed in the language. These terms were designed to make an individual, his family, and his possessions appear humble in the presence of the superior. In his relationships with inferiors, such as his sister, wife, or a merchant of lesser status, a man was permitted to be indifferent or even arrogant, although in general he was paternalistic.

The power of the Japanese family to teach these obligations and to extend them was shown forcefully to the world twenty-eight years after the end of World War II, when a Japanese corporal was found living in a cave on the island of Guam, still refusing to surrender. He was fulfilling a moral duty to the emperor, whose instructions to stop fighting he had never heard. For the same reasons Japanese kamikaze pilots crashed their bomb-laden planes into American ships during the war. Although they were destroyed in the process they were performing their obligations.

An *on* leading to death was a more dramatic form of the moral obligations which all Japanese experienced to some degree daily. The chart opposite this page shows the categories of people from whom an *on* may be received and the extent to which repayments must be made. The *on* received from the emperor is a continuing one that can never be repaid (*gimu*). The *on* due to parents, ancestors, and one's job are also in a similar category. In a lesser category are those which are repaid in proportion to what is received (*giri*). They may be responses to damaging as well as to helpful acts. For example, the receipt of an insult to one's name must be repaid—perhaps in the form of a duel—and repayment may be limited to a single act.

Because of the responsibility that it imposed, the Japanese became wary of accepting an *on*. Having to repay one to the emperor was burdensome but inevitable. To be compelled to assume one by an equal or an inferior was a humiliation that implied inferiority in the receiver. The Japanese therefore learned to look upon favors with suspicion, an attitude which surprised most foreigners. Assistance, even after an accident, was resented. In traditional society a talent, called a *tenbun* (literally, "allocation from Heaven"), was a gift that placed on its owner the responsibility for excellent performance.

SCHEMATIC TABLE OF
JAPANESE OBLIGATIONS AND THEIR RECIPROCALS*

I. *On:* obligations passively incurred. One receives an *on'*; one wears an *on,'* i.e., *on* are obligations from the point of view of the passive recipient.

> *ko on. On* received from the Emperor.
> *oya on. On* received from parents.
> *nushi no on. On* received from one's lord.
> *shi no on. On* received from one's teacher.
> *on* received in all contacts in the course of one's life.
> NOTE: All these persons from whom one receives *on* become one's *on jin,* '*on* man.'

II. Reciprocals of *on.* One 'pays' these debts, one 'returns these obligations' to the *on* man, i.e., these are obligations regarded from the point of view of active repayment.

> A. *Gimu.* The fullest repayment of these obligations is still no more than partial and there is no time limit.
> > *chu.* Duty to the Emperor, the law, Japan.
> > *ko.* Duty to parents and ancestors (by implication, to descendants).
> > *nimmu.* Duty to one's work.
>
> B. *Giri.* These debts are regarded as having to be repaid with mathematical equivalence to the favor received and there are time limits.
> > 1. *Giri*-to-the-world.
> > > Duties to liege lord.
> > > Duties to affinal family.
> > > Duties to non-related persons due to *on* received, e.g., on a gift of money, on a favor, on work contributed (as a 'work party').
> > > Duties to persons not sufficiently closely related (aunts, uncles, nephews, nieces) due to *on* received not from them but from common ancestors.
> >
> > 2. *Giri*-to-one's-name. This is a Japanese version of *die Ehre.*
> > > One's duty to 'clear' one's reputation of insult or imputation of failure, i.e., the duty of feuding or vendetta. (N.B. This evening of scores is not reckoned as aggression.)
> > > One's duty to admit no (professional) failure or ignorance.
> > > One's duty to fulfill the Japanese proprieties, e.g., observing all respectful behavior, not living above one's station in life, curbing all displays of emotion on inappropriate occasions, etc.

* From *The Chrysanthemum and the Sword,* by Ruth Benedict, published by Houghton Mifflin, Boston: reprinted by permission.

Moreover, it was not his to keep, but to hold in trust for future generations.

Unaware of the basis of these complex sensibilities, the rest of the world failed to understand the members of the tiny nation that had suddenly become a power. The Japanese strove to fulfill their obligations under all conditions. Whatever the cost of educating their children, parents would bear it in order to repay their debt to their own parents. A sister might hate her older brother yet steadfastly fulfill her obligations to him. These were conditions which created unhappiness. But the Japanese family did not exist to make its members happy. Its function was to perfect itself as a unit.

The family sought a goal that lay in the future rather than in the present: the honor of the family. This objective was one part of the Japanese belief in the honor and divinity of the Japanese people. As each member of the family sacrificed for the whole, so would each family sacrifice for Japan. Shintoism reinforced this concept. The Meiji leaders made that ancient faith a state religion after 1868. In 1884, they elevated it to a cult, superseding all others. They called it "Shrine Shinto." It had no god but Japan itself—the object of worship usually was a distant mountain that could be viewed from a simple shrine. It had no prayers or trappings—the chief decorations were strips of paper symbolizing the souls of famous Japanese heroes and of

Family occupational traditions exert a powerful influence over individual Japanese. Artisans particularly tend to continue their forefather's work.

other souls thought divine.

In its relationship with other countries, Japan sought to express the need for order, hierarchy, and national destiny, which were viewed as the central objectives of its people. To explain the invasion of China to its own people, the Japanese government pointed out that Japan had a responsibility to help the Chinese learn their place in the world order. While there were many other reasons for invading China, none was more compelling to the Japanese.

Japan announced that it was compelled to fight World War II because " . . . the present situation . . . runs directly counter to Japan's fundamental policy to enable each nation to enjoy its proper station in the world." Like most of its individuals, Japan regarded position as the chief, if not the sole basis for self-esteem.

THE LEGACY OF HISTORY

The Confucian basis of authority. To justify the degree of authority assigned to each member of the family, the leaders of Tokugawa Japan cited Confucianism. But China and Japan differed in their understanding of Confucian ideals. In the Chinese views, humans were part of the natural order, the elements of which interacted reciprocally. Authority rested in the head of the family, but he was to behave towards the family's other members in the spirit of *jen* (pronounced "ren," meaning "benevolence"). That is, he was to respect their individuality. The national authority culminated in the

Japanese society tends to form groups in which there are similar economic or educational backgrounds. This scene is above the port of Nagasaki.

emperor. Nevertheless, the people had a duty to withdraw it if it were shown that the emperor had lost the "Mandate of Heaven"—if he proved to be an ineffective ruler.

When transferred to Japan, these concepts were altered. The father was supreme in the family and the emperor in the nation. Neither could be questioned. As we have seen, by a tradition which long preceded the advent of Confucianism in Japan, the Japanese emperor was more than a "Son of Heaven," which the Chinese called their ruler. He was the personification of god on earth. People were not permitted to look upon him. When he passed, crowds would bow in unison or avert their eyes. When he asked it, some Japanese might willingly give their lives. His name was never mentioned. Yet throughout Japan the authority of every bureaucrat or army officer rested upon the general belief that "He speaks for the emperor."

The Tokugawa-Meiji heritage. The Tokugawa Shogunate secured internal peace for Japan at the cost of the discipline which it imposed. It was a thoroughly organized state. Every Japanese was expected to avoid colliding with others. Children were taught to control their aggressions by the age of three or four. Prizes were offered for piety and chastity. Conflicting groups were reminded of their obligations to the emperor. Through the publication of codes and placards, every individual was made aware of the need for hard work, thrift, and patriotism. Laws were designed to prevent the changing of jobs or lands.

In contrast to China, the Japanese developed a rigid hierarchy as a result of these disciplines. We have seen that, beneath the emperor, shogun, and the daimyo were the samurai and that beneath them were the people. Under the Tokugawa Shogunate each social level was granted respect to the extent of its status. Each would defer to the people on the social level above it. Even within the general population, or *heimin*, distinctions were clear. In this largest social level, the highest status was granted to the wealthiest landowners or to those closest to the daimyo. Artisans were ranked beneath the peasants; merchants, considered petty and corrupt handlers of money, were below them. Near the bottom of society were those whose occupations were said to pollute their bodies: actors, waitresses, geisha, prostitutes. The lowest of all were outcastes, similar to India's untouchables. This group (*Eta*) included the handlers of leather and garbage, butchers, undertakers, and night soil collectors.

Except for the Eta, who were condemned to their place for life, changes in rank were possible and perhaps were more common than in contemporary Europe. Education was the chief means by which upward mobility was achieved. As cities grew and the gulf between the holdings of the daimyo and the merchants narrowed, many sons of merchants were able to gain samurai status. Many others arranged to have their daughters married to samurai in order to associate themselves with the more esteemed caste.

The Meiji Restoration reformed Japanese society, economy, education, government, law, and military forces. Restrictions were removed on the transfer of land, residence, and occupation. Many peasants acquired land; and freed from the Tokugawa requirement that they keep their occupations, they retrained themselves. Drawn by industrialization, peasants increasingly migrated to cities. There, education was more readily available. The way was opened for families to advance by sending their sons to universities.

But the concept of rank had become instilled in Japanese life. Despite the Meiji reforms, Japan was in effect still controlled by the concept of hierarchy which its family life perpetuated. It took enormous wealth to attend the imperial universities. The government drew all of its officials from the law department of the leading university in Tokyo. The major businesses hired only university graduates or young men powerfully supported by a *kone*, a guarantor whose position was acceptable. An apprentice (*shosei*) system enabled some young men to advance if they could persuade trained professionals to sponsor them.

JAPAN IN TRANSITION

By the end of the occupation, visible changes had taken place in Japanese life. The reforms of the immediate postwar period accelerated trends that had been started by the growth of the money economy, industrialization, and urbanization. An individual's family and sex were of less importance to society; his associates and ability became more important. Traditional and modern or Western-influenced ways of life began to exist side-by-side.

The occupation required Japan to reevaluate a social system whose parts yielded submissively to the power of those above. We have seen that under the 1947 Constitution the emperor remained the symbol of Japanese unity, but was permitted no policymaking functions. At the same time, Japan officially declared individuals to be free, if they wished, from the burdensome obligations that had been imposed by the family.

There followed a breakdown of many traditional values. Some formal courtesy terms were dropped from the language. Yet, people were hesitant to be the first to not use these courteous forms. Newspapers would carry articles discussing the problems of change. One was headed, "How should we address sales-girls?" Most people were not sure whether to continue the practice of bowing to others. Confused by the new concept of equality, most could not decide which person should bow the longest or the deepest. In business, the

Japanese attempt to establish rank promptly by exchanging calling cards at the outset of a meeting. A glance at his caller's title enables the businessman to know how to behave.

The Japanese people accept the idea of equality. They are annoyed when it is violated, as when a large corporation wins special attention from government. On a day-to-day basis, however, their historical training may make them feel uncomfortable in the presence of inferiors or superiors. Often they form groups that arrange to separate people of different ranks. Professional organizations, such as those formed by doctors, lawyers, artists, and scientists, contain factions. Usually the factions are defined by the universities that were attended by their members. In most companies an individual's age, graduation date, or university affiliation will determine the faction to which he belongs. His social as well as his business contacts will fall within this group. Hamlets form associations which accept newcomers on the basis of a formal application, accompanied by a gift. Once he becomes a member of the association, the individual is expected to agree with the policies of the group.

While it helps people to classify others, education remains, as it was during the Tokugawa and Meiji periods, one of the principal ways to gain advancement. It is compulsory through the ninth grade. Beyond that level the student is likely to go to a school whose prestige is no greater than the prestige of his social class. Whether a young

Japanese students are aware that their position in society throughout their lives will be determined largely by the quality of their education.

Japanese will advance or remain in his father's position often depends chiefly on the university he attends. Tokyo and Kyoto Imperial universities are the most prestigious. Students try bravely to enter these schools, often taking the entrance examinations repeatedly, for as long as they can afford to continue. Of the students admitted to Tokyo University in a recent class, more than half took the examination more than once.

Because of the importance of education in the social structure, many parents begin to prepare their children for college at the age of six. Yet only about 40 percent of parents can afford to finance their children through the end of high school. All costs of high school, including books, transportation, food, and tuition, are borne by the families. Seeing their parents struggle with this burden, Japanese students generally do not need to be encouraged to work hard in school. They want to repay their debt. They know that success in school will be important to them for the rest of their lives.

Upon leaving a university, a graduate applies for a job and is quick to learn that his school's status will affect his career. In his interview he is likely to mention his family's status and friends. Probably he will find a *kone* to recommend him. In recent years, high school teachers and college professors have taken this role, guaranteeing the performance of their best students.

On the job, the young Japanese will experience further evidence that old and new ways of thinking exist simultaneously. He is likely to find that his associates have developed groups whose heads are foremen or other executives. He will join one, probably because it is made up of former students of his school. His group will maintain its cohesiveness through convivial meetings, favors granted by one member to another, and gifts which are not offered to outsiders. It will demand his loyalty and obedience. Parties are given in which mutual trust may be expressed through the consumption of alcoholic drinks. Drunkenness, even when pretended, is taken to imply confidence in those who witness it.

While the group develops this cohesiveness, it is also building a defensive wall against the outer world. Instead of competing as individuals, the members of each group see themselves competing with other groups. They tend to think of the other groups as threats to the security of their own. Because of the humiliation that it may cause the losers, individual competition is discouraged at all levels of life. Salary increases are given more to reward a group than its members. A quota may be given to the heads of each group, and they in turn disburse it.

The idea that people can be cooperative and considerate to the members of other groups has become stronger with the rise of the white-collar class. More individuals have gained the right to find personal happiness outside of their groups. Such universal ideas as peace and the brotherhood of man have captured the imaginations of millions of Japanese.

At the same time, the non-conformist in Japan often is accused of being "unfeeling." Opinions not represented by large groups may be considered suspect and radical. Elected officials are seen as father-figures whose authority is not to be questioned. Thus, while a vigorous movement of intellectuals and professionals is growing, ancient concepts persist, often taking new forms.

The enduring institution of the Japanese family remains, but its authority has come under challenge. Other groups, such as unions, factions, corporations, commercial associations, and political parties have tended to replace its authority. Nevertheless, behavior formerly practiced in the families today is being practiced in the new groups. Mutual obligations based on personal relationships continue to be compelling reasons for action. The hierarchy which governs the family is, often to a startling degree, evident in the other groups.

CHAPTER 10

INDEPENDENT JAPAN

JAPAN LOST MORE THAN THREE MILLION lives in World War II, and more than a quarter of the nation's industry was destroyed. Every major city was in ruins; the country was near starvation. Yet today, there is little to remind visitors that a war ever took place. Tourists are impressed with the neon glitter of such rebuilt metropolises as Tokyo and Osaka. The acceptance of the cruder Western institutions (such as soft drinks, baseball, pin-ball machines, jazz, and rock-and-roll) gives the impression that the experiment in Asian democracy has been a smashing success.

The Japanese standard of living is among the twenty highest in the world. Only the United States and Russia out-produce Japan. The astonishing recovery of the defeated nation may be credited to two factors. One was the willingness of the victors to supply assistance, valued at more than three billion dollars. The other, and of greater importance, was the skill and energy with which the Japanese applied themselves to the problems of reconstruction. They have driven themselves with what has seemed to the world to be a single purpose—national prosperity. Their efforts were fruitful from the very beginning. By the late 1960's Japan's economy was expanding at the rate of more than ten percent a year—double or triple the rate of the United States. Some economists have predicted that by the 1980's the per capita income in Japan will exceed that of the United States. Vast accumulations of capital have taken place inside of Japan. They are due both to increasing profits and to the willingness of most families to save. With the economic tide turning, the Japanese have been able to invest in other countries—throughout Europe and Asia and, ironically, in the United States, which only a short time ago was their main source of funds.

Japan's economy is not as healthy as it appears on the surface. With the loss of Korea, Manchuria, and the holdings in China, she is today obliged to import almost all of her raw materials (coking coal, oil, iron ore, and raw cotton, for example). To bring them to her ports and then to carry her manufactured products back to the world's markets, she has often had to ship more than half of the world's maritime tonnage. Nor is domestic food production sufficient for the rising demand. Despite heroic efforts by Japanese farmers to increase yields from the land, food imports have risen to one fifth of the total food consumed.

Nevertheless, Japan has stunned the world by solving these problems—at least for the present. Her success is due to her ability to win a larger percentage of the world markets for her manufactured exports. Careful purchasing of raw materials and brilliant efficiency in her manufacturing industries have yielded products of high quality. In such fields as optics, electronics, and office machines her merchandise has steadily gained acceptance. Often it has replaced the products of West German, French, English, and American companies. Japan now ranks second among nations in the production of electronics equipment. She is third in the production of motor vehicles. Her growing commerce has brought her full employment; students are often signed up for jobs long before they are graduated; and newcomers to the labor market may be offered as many as four jobs.

Japan is a crowded nation, with more than 107,000,000 people living in an area slightly smaller than the state of California. However, the population problem is less pressing than it seemed to be

With an increasing population and limited land, Japanese farmers have been forced to invent ways to use sloping terrain and air space for crops.

In less than 20 years Japan has become a major world auto producer.

immediately after World War II. In 1947, the birth rate was 34 per thousand people. By 1957, a birth-control program, including inexpensive, legalized abortions and the distribution of contraceptives, reduced the rate to 17 per thousand. Today, Japan's population growth is about one percent per year, which is the rate in many Western countries. Japanese families have readily accepted birth control as a means of achieving goals they consider of primary importance for their children—high income and thorough education.

Thus the postwar years have brought rapid economic and social changes—more rapid than had been achieved in the previous century. The trend was toward far greater material progress for all. Postwar despair, which caused many Japanese to lose faith in their government, has been replaced by optimism. Material success has restored Japanese pride. But growth has also brought severe strains. Japan, whose per capita income now exceeds that of most Western countries, has become the first Asian nation to emerge completely into modern times. Her chief problems now are therefore not economic but political.

The cities. New smokestacks have been raised into Japan's urban skies. Japan tripled its steel production from 1955 to 1961, when its output was 29.5 million tons. By 1972, its steel production had surpassed that of the United States. In the same postwar period it tripled its production of all manufactured goods and doubled its

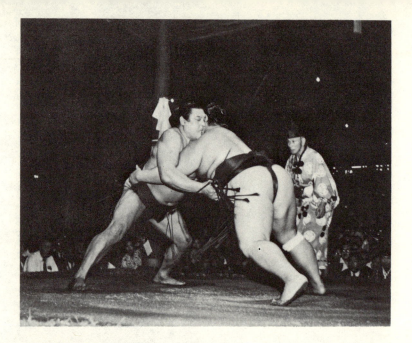

With increasing leisure time, millions of Japanese are attending sporting events. This is sumo, a 2,000-year-old form of wrestling.

electrical power. The stream of products from Japanese assembly lines has had a profound impact on the lives of the urban Japanese.

The new prosperity has swept aside ancient traditions. Old customs, dress, and speech are being forgotten in the rush for products. It has been said that until recently the most treasured items in any Japanese household were the sword, the jewel, and the mirror. Today, these have been replaced by the washing machine, the refrigerator, and the television set. The ancient cities are choked with cars. Millions of Japanese have become addicted to Western-style clubs and associations, to golf, jazz, and skiing. *How to Improve Your English* has been one of Japan's most popular books of the past decade.

These changes are more than superficial copying of the American desires and customs. On the contrary, Japan is an urban civilization in its own right. She exhibits tendencies that usually accompany a nation's passage from the agricultural into the industrial age, but they are uniquely Japanese. Millions of Japanese have left their agricultural society to cluster in cities. The cities now contain more than 70 percent of the country's population. More than 10 percent of all Japanese now live in Tokyo, and 33 percent in four industrial centers on the Pacific Ocean. Tokyo, whose population reached 11 million in the 1960's, is the largest city in the world.

In every Japanese city there has been frantic construction to accommodate newcomers. Hundreds of suburbs have been expanded or created, often with concrete buildings four to six stories high, containing small apartments. Shopping centers have been developed and stuffed with goods. Much as they do in the United States, people worry about how to spend their leisure time. Beaches are crowded and sports activities well attended. There is deep concern throughout Japan over the pollution of air and water, the disposal of human and industrial wastes, and the rising crime rate.

The cities have other problems characteristic of rapid growth. Many areas were poorly planned as the country's wealth and population increased. The construction of libraries, hospitals, utilities, and other public buildings has lagged behind the need for them. But Japanese workers are well paid and seem content. Although there is an annual debate over wages, usually ending with increases of about 10 percent to workers in the newer industries, employees often keep their jobs for life. In the paternalistic Japanese economy they are often paid on the basis of their loyalty and their way of life, rather than because of how they produce. This, plus the fact that many businesses treat their employees as though they were members of a family, tends to blunt the arguments of militants in the labor movement.

The country. Conservative Japanese governments have carefully served the interests of the nation's farmers. Although the rural

At night the Shinjuki Station Square, one of Tokyo's busiest commercial centers, reflects the increasingly modern quality in most Japanese cities.

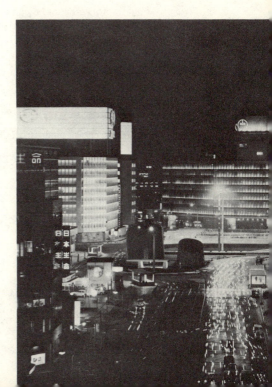

population is shrinking, its political support is more dependable than that of the large urban groups. As a result, it has gained price supports and subsidies, particularly for rice; thus it has had more income to distribute among fewer people. New houses and equipment are visible throughout Japan's rural areas. Japanese farmers and their families are among the crowds of Japanese tourists who now travel to the West during each vacation season.

Japanese farms are small; land is used as completely as possible. Before World War II, Japan was growing food as it always had, with manual labor and a few farm animals. The end of the war saw the introduction of insecticides, chemical fertilizers, and machines which greatly expanded the yield per acre. However, as noted above, the country produces only about four fifths of the food that it needs. One reason is that it is beginning to use more high-protein foods, such as meat, milk, and wheat, which are not widely produced in Japan. Rice is plentiful, however, and remains Japan's largest crop.

Political groups. During the occupation, the Japanese were encouraged to revive parties that had been suppressed by militarists. After extended competition for popular support, these parties resolved themselves into two conservative and two "socialist" camps. The socialists formed a single party in 1955, causing the conservatives to unify, too. This action is what led to the creation of the Liberal Democratic Party.

The one-man tractor, powered by gasoline, has enabled many of Japan's farmers to achieve amazingly high yields from relatively small plots.

After the war, conservatism was often identified with the government that had engineered the disastrous policy of expansion. Socialists won widespread support, particularly among intellectuals, because they seemed to provide the only clear alternative to the defeated militarists. To their left on the political spectrum, the Communists gained some popularity for the same reason. It was never extensive, however; the votes cast for Japan's Communist Party have been limited to from three to ten percent of the total.

Although the position of left-wing parties against warfare has appealed to most Japanese, their connections in Russia and China have aroused fears. The Japanese regard both Russia and China as economic competitors or political adversaries. A sizable part of the urban vote has gone to the right wing because of this issue. The business community and bureaucracy have also kept their traditional alliance with conservatives. When combined with conservative rural voters, these blocs have been large enough to keep the Liberal Democratic Party in power.

The political strength of the conservatives is not based on national party ideology alone, but also on the personal relationships that have been formed between conservatives and the electorate. Like American congressmen, the members of the Japanese Diet represent small regions where they are known as individuals as well as political figures. They must please their constituency if they want to be re-elected. But when they are functioning in the Diet, away from home, they must please their party, which extends political rewards to them if they cooperate. The system leaves room for vigorous disputes over party loyalty, faithful representation, and personal ambition. There is much maneuvering for political control. The trading for better positions goes on continuously.

While large numbers of businessmen, farmers, and bureaucrats support the Liberal Democrats, the Socialists have a large following among educators, students, and professionals. The Sohyo, a union of government employees and other white collar workers, generally favors Socialist candidates. Blue collar unions have chiefly economic goals and support either Socialists or Communists to achieve them. These blocs of voters all are opposed to Liberal Democratic policies that tend to raise prices by subsidizing farmers. Yet they rarely agree on a united program.

In recent years a fourth party has arisen to claim votes from both the right and the left. It is the Komeito ("Clean Politics" Party), which represents the more militant members of the urban lower class. Highly disciplined, the Komeito Party is associated with a "new religion." It stems from the teachings of Nichiren, the thirteenth-century Buddhist who urged his followers to become aggressive nationalists. On national issues its program is conservative. On international ones, such as peace, it is more like the Socialist Party.

The progress of the Japanese economy has produced two other political forces in recent years. One is made up of students, a group that is increasingly isolated from the views of traditional Japan. Many students are uncompromisingly Marxist. Heeding Marx's belief that war and poverty are results of capitalism, they have called peace and a greater distribution of wealth their primary objectives. Paradoxically, they have often used violence in the effort to achieve them. Through a group called the Zengakuren, in the late 1950's they protested every association of Japan with the United States. By the 1960's, this group had broken into three parts which fought each other as well as the national government. It seized and damaged whole universities, particularly when the United States began to increase its role in the Vietnam war. Since there was resistance to the use of police on campuses, the Diet induced the schools themselves to control rebellious students. It cut the faculty pay where riots took place. This, the reduction of fighting in Southeast Asia, and the gradual withdrawal of the United States from Japan, have diminished the riots, both in number and scope.

A second political force created by the new prosperity is made up of the workers and entrepreneurs who are not directly part of the modern Japanese economy. They are often "temporary" workers who move from job to job among companies that are employed by the

Multi-storied concrete apartment houses, recently constructed in Japanese suburbs, are tending to change traditional ways of thinking.

Although it is seemingly unified in its goals, Japan is made up of diverse groups which contribute vigorously to political dialogues

big corporations, or the shopkeepers who own their own businesses. They do not receive the benefits of paternalistic companies and make their own way in the swiftly moving society. They form the second part of what sociologists have called Japan's "dual economy." While they have no predictable political cause, they are united by circumstances and form a potential voting bloc in Japanese politics.

Thus there are sharp divisions in Japanese society. They are not revealed by a superficial glance at the country's prosperity. Businessmen, students, intellectuals, unions, laborers, farmers, the urban classes, and the secondary group of workers and entrepreneurs are often strikingly opposed to one another.

Government policies. Within twenty years after hostilities ceased, Japan began to show signs of reverting to its prewar conservatism. Economic combines broken by the occupation forces began to re-form. Though the largest Japanese industrial firms are being run on American management lines instead of being dominated by single families, the zaibatsu regained much of their old influence.

More significant regressions took place in the post war management of Japanese educational and police systems. They indicated Japan's deeper questions about democracy. In 1954, the administration of Prime Minister Yoshida placed teachers under the control of the national government in order to silence their criticism. This reversed a decision of the occupation authorities to put education under local control. Almost at the same time, a struggle for Japanese civil liberties developed when Yoshida moved to bring the police under national control, too.

To counter Yoshida, the Socialists in the House of Representatives filibustered in order to postpone any decision on the nationalization of police. But Yoshida, over the riotous protests of the Socialists, managed to extend the life of the legislative session and so to defeat the filibuster. This caused the Socialists to boycott the rest of the session. Their antagonists approved the police bill without them. A National Police Reserve of 75,000 men was formed to replace American occupation troops who were ordered into the Korean War. Thus, for the first time since World War II, Japan moved toward the development of an army, however small and "defensive."

Although many Westerners thought that Yoshida moved too fast in a conservative direction, his supporters contended that he was not moving fast enough to undo the reforms of the immediate post-war period. Domestic strife was further exacerbated when fallout from an American nuclear test in the mid-Pacific killed a Japanese fisherman. The administration was compelled by angry demonstrators to defend its American alliance. When the so-called Liberal Party decided to withdraw support from his administration, Yoshida resigned in December, 1954. A political crisis swept all Japan. It was at this point that the Socialists united and the Liberals joined the equally misnamed Progressive Party to form the Liberal Democratic Party.

Soon this coalition elected a new prime minister, Hatoyama Ichiro. The constitution reflected American culture more than it did the Japanese, it said. It proposed amendments that would have undone much of the work of the occupation authorities.

First, the coalition proposed that full sovereign power be restored to the emperor. The Diet did not confirm a constitutional amendment to that effect, but this became less necessary as the emperor was consulted more and more. The Liberal Democrats also moved to strengthen the National Police Reserve. In 1954, the Reserve gained a small navy and air force. A "Self-Defense Agency" was formed. Two years later the conservatives eliminated the constitutional provision for the election of school board members. Instead, the Ministry of Education began to appoint and to regulate them.

Although the Socialists and Communists often protested these changes through demonstrations and in the Diet, they were unable to rally enough popular support to stop the conservative actions. The Socialists have rarely attracted more than a third of the votes cast in any election. They remained a minority party, despite their alliance.

By 1957, conservative strength had become so great that a man who held office in the Japanese government that planned World War II was elected prime minister. This man, Kishi Nobusuke, had been tried for war crimes by SCAP, but was acquitted. As prime minister, he restored several military men to office. Kishi faced his severest test in 1960, when President Eisenhower was planning to visit Japan to conclude the renegotiations of the U.S.-Japanese Security Treaty of 1952.

The security treaty authorized the United States to move troops to Japan, either to defend the country or its region against invasion or "to put down large-scale internal riots and disturbances." Many Japanese, particularly the Socialists and Communists, regarded this clause as an abrogation of national rights. In one of their most persuasive arguments they stated that because the treaty had no terminal date, Japan was little more than an American colony, subject to American military control at any time.

When the treaty was signed in 1952, Japan feared the growing power of China, which had recently become Communist, and of Russia, which was refusing to sign a peace treaty. By 1958, however, it was much stronger, both economically and militarily. The renegotiation that Kishi arranged limited the treaty to ten years. During this period the United States could use Japanese bases only if Japan consented.

As plans were made to sign the treaty, an American U-2 "spy plane" was shot down over Russia. This forced the cancellation of a meeting that President Eisenhower was to have had with Russia's premier, Nikita Khrushchev. In an atmosphere of crisis, Kishi met increasing opposition to the conclusion of the treaty. However, in order to gain the government's support of the agreement in time for Eisenhower's visit, he arranged for an early morning vote in the Diet. The Socialists responded with a call to protest. Angered over what they considered a betrayal by Kishi, hundreds of thousands of Japanese, of all ages and classes, demonstrated in the streets. Police action did little more than infuriate the crowds. Thoroughly embarrassed, Kishi told Eisenhower that his trip to Japan could be dangerous. Although the treaty was later ratified, the visit was canceled, to the humiliation of the Liberal Democrats and many other Japanese.

In their reaction to the treaty, the demonstrators were joined by a common rage. Many Japanese have dreaded war, in a more deep-seated way than people of other nations, since that stunning moment when the United States airmen dropped an atomic bomb on their city of Hiroshima. Many have mistrusted the United States since then, claiming that Americans must despise Asians to have been willing to destroy 100,000 mostly non-military citizens in one stroke. The fact that American immigration laws still discriminated against Asians and that American planes later conducted high-altitude bombing of Vietnam did little to diminish this belief.

After the riots in 1960, Premier Kishi resigned in favor of another conservative but pro-Western statesman, Ikeda Hayato. Cam-

The Tokkaido Line, which runs the 320 miles between Tokyo and Osaka at speeds up to 125 miles per hour, is the world's fastest train.

paigning on promises to increase prosperity, Ikeda, a former finance minister, won two two-year terms. He more than fulfilled his pledge. By the end of his tenure, the country was producing as much as all the rest of Asia. Japan's attention thus was shifted from international to national issues. In 1964, Ikeda was succeeded by Sato Eisaku, who was elected for three consecutive terms. The nation's energies were chiefly directed to preparations for the Olympic Games, for which she was to be host, in that year. Proudly, Japan displayed to the world transportation and communications systems that had no equal. Subways, elevated roads, and a "supertrain"—the Tokaido Railway—were built for the occasion.

In 1969, the dispute over the American alliance, which underlay all foreign policy debates in Japan, rose violently to the surface. The issue was the Pacific island of Okinawa, a Japanese prefecture which the United States had been using as a military base since 1945. To the dismay of the proud Japanese, the Americans were governing more than a million of their countrymen on the island and others in the Ryukyu group. Calls for the repossession of Okinawa brought no action from the conservative Japanese government. On the other hand, the United States regarded its Okinawa air base as vital to the defense of all of the Pacific, including Japan.

The United States resolved some of the tension over this issue by agreeing to acknowledge Japanese ownership of Okinawa. However, it did so under the provisions of the Security Treaty. This permitted it to continue to use its air base on Okinawa as long as it had the consent of the Japanese government. By 1972, the island was formally restored to Japan. Since American military personnel remained there, this gesture did not go far enough for many militant Japanese.

In 1964 the Japanese were the proud hosts for athletes of the 94 nations participating in the largest Olympic Games in world history.

Nevertheless, Sato's conclusion of the Okinawa treaty did help him to win a third two-year term. In 1972, he was replaced by Tanaka Kakuei, another Liberal Democrat.

PRESENT POLICIES

Premier Tanaka had been a foot soldier in the Japanese army during the invasion of China. Fully aware of the revival of China as an economic force in Asia, he moved swiftly after his election to regain a peaceful relationship with the mainland. Flying to Peking, he was greeted coolly but cordially by Mao Tse-tung and Chou En-lai. Tanaka apologized profusely for the "past offenses" of Japanese troops in China. His efforts were rewarded with the opening of more extensive diplomatic and commercial relationships.

China holds a special place in the minds of most Japanese. It is the source of culture—the "old country" which produced many Asian civilizations, including their own. Japan is conscious of the fact that the United States may not always be its primary trading partner. She looks to China as an alternative. The vast markets on the mainland provide a handy place to sell many goods that are not yet produced efficiently there, such as electronics equipment. China is an excellent source of goods that the Japanese cannot produce in large enough quantities, such as textiles. Japan was China's best customer in 1973, with a two-way trade of more than one billion dollars.

These are powerful reasons why the two countries are likely to develop a livelier commercial and cultural exchange. But Japan is wary of, as well as attracted to China. The giant population on the mainland could produce an overwhelming military force. China has the atomic bomb. Nuclear explosions on remote Chinese deserts have produced a fallout that has seemed dangerous to some Japanese scientists. This development in their Communist neighbor has weakened the arguments of Japanese who opposed American nuclear testing.

Japan's attitude toward the United States is a complex mixture of admiration, gratitude, and resentment. On the one hand, the Japanese are aware that the Americans were generous with them at the conclusion of World War II. American advice and material aid were unsparing. The United States provided the economic model for what Japan yearned to become, a thoroughly industrialized nation well into the electronic and nuclear age. American nuclear power protected the Japanese, freeing them from the need to build their defenses.

But to many Japanese, the Americans have been an obstacle to their more complete development and independence. A people as conscious of self-esteem as the Japanese cannot help wanting American soldiers, planes, and ships to leave their soil. Although the Americans maintain their bases in Japanese territory to protect Japanese as well as American interests, there is a growing feeling in Japan that the need for defense has diminished. A large number of left-wing Japanese, moreover, regard Americans as the leaders of the capitalist world that they are pledged to change. This group saw the Vietnam war as further evidence of Americans intentions to restrain Asia.

Visiting Peking,
Premier Tanaka toasted
Chou En-lai of the
People's Republic of China.

Fortunately, the United States also sees the modern world in more peaceful terms than was possible immediately after World War II. Its cessation of nuclear testing in the Pacific, its ultimate withdrawal of troops after the agonizing conflict in Vietnam, and its restoration of Okinawa to Japan all are evidence of willingness to recognize the emergence of Asia. Its own long-range weapons system tends to preclude the need for bases in remote parts of the Pacific.

While the United States probably wants to avoid confrontations with Japan and other Asian countries, it may prove unable to continue in the positive role that is has played. More than one third of the raw materials needed by Japan have been imported from the United States, which, however, spends much more in Japan than it earns there. Trade between the two countries exceeds seven billion dollars a year—the largest transoceanic trade in history. But American raw materials, such a lumber and oil, have been in short supply, and American expenditures abroad have been eroding its economy. Probably the United States will be forced to cut back on Japanese imports, either because their prices will increase or because it will be unable to continue spending abroad at past levels.

The Japanese government has put brakes on its shipments to the United States, hoping to alleviate the drain on its trading partner before it gets worse. At all costs, Japan wants to avoid forcing the United States to erect tariff barriers around its products—a move that could start similar actions around the world. Therefore, it has begun to limit the export of some goods, particularly those which threaten to damage American industries. Slowly, it is being forced to allow more American goods into Japan, thus permitting the United States to send competitive products, as well as raw materials, to its domestic markets. This tendency, when combined with rising wages and military budgets in Japan, is certain to adjust the trading positions of the two countries.

Recognizing the importance of its relationship with the United States, Japan's Liberal Democratic Party has tended to build a foreign policy that was either neutral or favorable to the Americans. It opposed the recognition of Communist China and the admission of China to the United Nations, while continuing its recognition of the Republic of China. Japan's Socialists had been urging that the country build a better relationship with the mainland and argued that the United States alone interfered with this move. Having defended themselves against this charge, the conservatives were shocked when President Nixon unexpectedly visited Peking in 1972 to prepare closer diplomatic and commercial ties with the mainland. It was at this point that Sato, facing severe criticism of members of his own party, resigned and was replaced by Tanaka.

In its new affluence, Japan has attempted to help in the

The Yawata Iron and Steel Mill is Asia's largest center of ferrous industry. In 10 years Japan's crude steel production has increased 2½ times.

development of the rest of Asia. She has paid reparations for damages suffered during the war to Burma, the Philippines, Indonesia, and South Vietnam. To former colonies, such as Korea, she has extended loans and additional trade. To help in the general recovery of her region she gave $200 million to the Asian Development Bank—as much as the United States and a sum equal to one third of the total funds available—when the bank was founded in 1965.

Japan has also greatly improved her relations with Russia. Although the dispute over the ownership of the southern Kuriles continues, there has been an increase of trade between the two countries, and Russia has been considering a commercial partnership with Japan, under which her remote regions of Siberia would be developed on a large scale. Under this proposal, vast deposits of natural gas, coal, and oil would be jointly explored.

There is a negative side to Japanese success, however. Hidden beneath the surface of the nation's prosperity, it burst violently to the surface in 1974 in the form of criticism of the Japanese throughout Southeast Asia. Severe riots took place in Indonesia. There, eleven persons were killed and almost a thousand were arrested during demonstrations surrounding a state visit by Premier Tanaka. The Indonesians, reflecting views expressed in Thailand, the Philippines, Singapore, and Malaysia, held that Japanese investments were turning Indonesia into a colony of Japan. Japanese tourists, they said, had become arrogant and demanding, seeking to use their new-found wealth to change the way of life in other countries.

Premier Tanaka was visibly shaken at the unexpected hostility in neighboring countries. On his return home he gave a national television address to his people in which he said:

> *We must give ear humbly to reasonable criticisms against Japan, correct what we should correct, and improve our mutual relationships with a long-range perspective. . . . Japan will be unable to contribute to the establishment of a continuous peace in Asia unless Japan becomes a good friend of Asian nations by refraining from judging others by its own standards and by sharing both joys and hardships. . . . One hundred million Japanese, in a homogeneous race, have been able to concentrate their energies totally upon restoring and constructing our nation. At the same time, this has resulted in the Japanese having made much to reconsider and to study in terms of international cooperation and association with foreign nations. Our insular posture in pursuing our national interests could have been overlooked or justified to some extent during the process of recovering from the devastation of World War II. But today, that posture is not only unwarranted internationally, but very well may cause trouble.*

There is an abundant supply of food in Japan, but prices have risen rapidly. Prosperity is due to the country's increasing world economic role.

Pollution has become one of the major issues in Japanese politics. The country's sudden advances in manufacturing have damaged air, water and land.

The future of Japanese democracy. Despite a tendency to retreat from its democratic constitution, Japan has developed powerful forces that are certain to resist any return to militarism. She publishes more books, magazines, and newspapers than ever. This free press, now supplemented by two public and five private television networks, constantly generates ideas and change. Her population is entirely literate and better educated than ever before.

Gains by minority parties have prevented the ultraconservatives from further crippling the constitution, for such amendments require a two-thirds majority of the Diet. Further, the new freedom of Japanese womanhood is a force that must be reckoned with in postwar Japan. Japan's women are a formidable obstacle to a return to traditional ways. Lastly, Japanese youth, exposed to democracy, however fragmentary, relishes its new freedom and individualism. It will not return to servitude without a struggle. The student movement has an element that tends to be rash and counterproductive, but the youth of Japan are, in general, alert to the demands of responsible citizenship in a democracy.

The fragile Japanese democracy will no doubt be sustained if it is not pressed. Threats to the national interest tend to damage it. When threatened, Japan coheres. In her international relations she is rapidly moving into a position of greater independence and activity. From the end of the war until recently, Japan spent less than one percent of her gross national product on the military. This is less than 20 percent of the military budgets of many Western countries. The relatively small expenditure for defense has been an important factor in her economic recovery. It will rise rapidly, however, as the United States withdraws from Asia. Her military budget will be the seventh largest in the world by 1977.

In addition to this increasing capital outlay for non-productive purposes, the nation must pay the ecological costs of expansion. Frenzied industrialization has sometimes menaced life itself. In Tokyo, police must resort to the use of oxygen masks while directing heavy traffic. The nation was stunned recently when residents of Minamota, a coastal village, were poisoned by mercury in their fish. Some of the stricken villagers sued local industries and won the

Serene above a vital country, Mount Fuji glows in the last light of day.

equivalent of $3 million in court. It was the first major test of laws governing pollution, and it was certain to have far-reaching effects on Japanese industry.

Premier Tanaka's program for improving the quality of Japanese life has been a bold one. He proposed that tens of thousands of people be moved from crowded cities to outlying regions. He suggested that industries be concentrated away from centers of population and that workers be transported to them. Although the plan has captured the imaginations of many Japanese, its high cost has prevented its development. Tanaka's popularity has suffered as a result, but he has pledged himself to persuading business to spend more for the improvement of the environment.

To solve her domestic problems, Japan needs a peaceful world. As the economic leader of all non-Western nations, she provides a stunning example of material progress that has been gained, in large measure, by the sacrifice of other values. Her achievements are more than economic—she has great influence in the arts as well as in nations in order to prevent conflicts. Thus, a little more than two centuries after Commodore Perry sailed into Tokyo Bay and less than 30 years after World War II, Japan, more than any other Asian nation, can be said to have emerged from the feudal age. How her growing power will develop and be used remains a question about which all the world wonders.

APPENDIX A

Most Populous Nations

Source: United Nations Statistical Office

COUNTRY	Midyear Estimate (in Thousands)	Annual % Increase (1963-70) *	Density per Sq. Mi.	Area in Sq. Mi.	COUNTRY	Midyear Estimate (in Thousands)	Annual % Increase (1963-70) *	Density per Sq. Mi.	Area in Sq. Mi.
Communist China	759,619	1.8	304.9	3,690,546	Mexico	50,670	3.5	100.9	761.402
India	550,376	2.5	654.7	1,261,482	Philippines	38,493	3.5	494.3	115,800
USSR	242,800	1.1	42.5	8,647,249	Thailand	35,814	3.1	270.2	198,404
UNITED STATES	205,395	1.2	84.9	3,614,254	Turkey	35,232	2.5	366.7	301,302
Indonesia	121,198	2.8	315.3	575,743	Spain	33,290	1.0	261.4	194,833
Pakistan	114,189	2.1	467.1	365,432	Poland	32,805	1.0	405.3	120.693
Japan	103,539	1.1	1083.4	142,744	United Arab Republic	33,329	2.5	127.4	386,540
Brazil	95,305	3.2	42.5	3,294,110	Republic of Korea	31,793	2.4	1247.8	38,012
Nigeria	55,074	2.5	227.7	365,574	Iran	28,662	2.9	65.6	636,128
West Germany	59,554	1.0	936.4	95,727	Burma	27,584	2.2	158.3	261,720
United Kingdom	55,711	0.5	880.3	94,200	Ethiopia	25,046	1.9	78.7	471,653
Italy	53,667	0.8	639.3	116,272	Argentina	24,352	1.5	34.7	1,071,879
France	50,775	0.9	359.1	211,152	North Vietnam	21,154	2.4	513.4	61,277

* Projected population figure.

APPENDIX B

Guide to the Pronunciation of Japanese Words

Japanese. a (ah), e (eh), i (ee), o (oh), u (uh): The dipthongs, including ae, ai, oi, and ui, are treated as separate vowels, with the emphasis on the first letter. Consonants are pronounced almost as in English, with the major exception that the "r" is close to the English "l." Stress is slight or does not exist.

APPENDIX C

GLOSSARY

Ainu (eye-noo)—Early inhabitants of Japan who have Caucasian features.

Amaterasu-O-mi-kami (ah-mah-teh-rah-soo oh-me-kah-me)—Japanese Sun Goddess, the direct ancestor of the Emperor, according to Shintoists.

bakufu (bah-koo-foo)—The military government of Japan during the feudal period.

Bunuraku (bun-oo-rah-koo)—The traditional puppet theater.

banzai (bahn-sai)—The traditional Japanese cry of or for victory: "Ten thousand years—forever!"

buraku (boo-rah-koo)—A village.

Bushido (boo-she-doe)—"The Way of the Warrior," a code which became a model for behavior, principally for samurai, in Tokugawa Japan.

butsudan (but-soo-dahn)—In Buddhist homes, a shelf containing symbols of family ancestors and deity.

Confucius (con-few-shas)—The Latin form of the name Kung Fu-tse (joong-foo-dzah), the great philosopher of China's Chou Dynasty period.

daimyo (daym-yo)—Feudal lords during Japan's shogunate period.

Edo (ed-do)—Site of modern Tokyo.

emakimono (ee-mah-kee-moh-noh)—Japanese picture scrolls of the Kamakura period.

Eta (ee-tah)—The lowest Japanese class.

Gautama Siddhartha (GAU-tamah SID-harth-ah)—The prince later called Buddha, founder of the great philosophical religion, Buddhism, in India.

Genro (jen-roh)—Japanese Privy Council, comprised of powerful supporters of the Meiji Restoration.

gohei (goh-hee)—Paper strips symbolizing offerings to the Shinto gods.

haiku (hi-koo)—A seventeen-syllable poem, unrhymed and arranged in lines of 5-7-5.

hara kari (hara-kah-ree)—Suicide by disembowelment, practiced by a few Japanese after extreme humiliation.

Heian (hay-ahn)—The period of Japanese history (784–1185) when the capital was at Heian, now Kyoto.

hiragana (here-ah-gahna)—A cursive form of rendering Chinese characters which were borrowed to create the Japanese written language.

Issei (ees-ay)—A Japanese who moves to the United States.

Izanagi-Izanami (ehzah-nahgee—ehzah-nahmee)—Japanese god and goddess, the representatives and the male and female principles.

Jomon (joe-mon)—Early Japanese culture, characterized in pottery by a decoration resembling the rope pattern to which the word refers.

Kabuki (kab-oo-kee)—The traditional Japanese theater, in which stylized singing and dancing are offered.

Kamakura (kama-koo-rah)—The shogunate that began feudalism in Japan (1186–1333).

kami (kah-me)—A spirit or natural force, worshipped in Shinto shrines.

kampaku (kam-pah-koo)—A regent appointed during the rise of the Fujiwara for a Japanese emperor who did not wish to rule.

kana (kah-nah)—Japanese use of "borrowed names," in which Chinese characters stand for 48 Japanese sounds.

kanji (kahn-gee)—Numerous Chinese characters borrowed by the Japanese to express complete uninflected words in writing.

kirisute gomen (kih-rih-soo-tah go-men)—The right of Japanese samurai to slay a peasant for disrespect.

Kuroshio (kooro-she-ah)—The Japanese warm current, which flows northward from the Philippine Sea.

Kyoto (kio-tow)—An ancient capital of Japan, on the island of Honshu.

magatama (mah-gah-te-ma)—Prehistoric "curved jewels" made by Japanese from stone, bone, and horn.

Mahayana (mah-ha-yah-na)—The form of Buddhism which deified Gautama Buddha and suggests that in every age spiritual beings exist to help individuals gain salvation.

Manyoshu (mahn-yoh-shoo)—An anthology of Japanese verse compiled at the end of the Nara period.

Meiji (may-jeh)—"Enlightened rule": the restoration of imperial power in Japan, beginning in 1868.

Minamoto (min-ah-mo-toe)—The family which established the Kamakura Shogunate in 1192 A.D.

Mitsubishi (mit-soo-be-she)—One of the families forming the economic trust called the zaibatsu in Japan.

Mitsui (mit-soo-e)—A powerful Japanese family of the zaibatsu.

Muromachi (moo-roh-mach-ee)—Japanese period (1392–1573) in which the Ashikaga family dominated the nation.

Nichiren (nee-che-ren)—Founder of the Lotus sect of Japanese Buddhism.

Nisei (nee-say)—A child of Japanese ancestry born in another country, usually the United States.

No (no)—A highly-stylized form of Japanese dance-drama. (Also Noh.)

nusa (noo-sah)—Paper strips tied to posts in the Shinto purification ritual.

oyabun-kobun (oh-yah-bun-ko-bun)—The relation of employer to employe, meaning literally "parent to child."

Oyashio (o-yah-she-o)—The cold current that moves down from the north along the Japanese coast.

renga (ren-gah)—A style of Japanese poetry using linked couplets.

ronin (ro-nin)—Unemployed samurai who became free agents with the destruction of Japan's feudal system.

samurai (sah-moor-rye)—The warrior class of feudal Japan.

Sengoku (sen-go-koo)—Japan's medieval period (1534-1615).

shiki (she-key)—The land rights enjoyed by peasants in feudal Japan.

shikken (shik-ken)—A regent appointed for a shogun too young to rule.

Shinto (shin-toe)—The ancient Japanese religion that stresses the worship of nature.

shoen (shown)—The manor controlled by a court aristocrat in feudal Japan.

shogun (show-gun)—The title given to the feudal lord who controlled Japan in place of the emperor between 1185 and 1868.

Sumitomo (soo-me-toe-mo)—A great Japanese family, one of the zaibatsu.

sumo (soo-mah)—The legendary form of wrestling, still practiced, in which men weighing 200-300 pounds attempt to throw each other down on or out of a 15-foot ring.

Susa-no-wo (soo-sah-no-woe)—The brother of the Sun Goddess who was given the rule of the underworld.

Taiho (tie-hoe)—Japanese legal codes which reorganized the government ca. 702 A.D.

Taika (tie-kah)—Japanese economic and political reforms ca. 645 A.D.

Tenno (ten-o)—"Born of Heaven," title given to emperor.

Theravada (there-ah-vah-da)—The form of Buddhism which stresses personal salvation and Gautama Buddha's mortal nature; derisively called "Hinayana" ("Lesser Way") by some Mahayana Buddhists.

Tokugawa (toe-koo-gah-wah)—The ruling family in Japan from 1603-1867.

tozama (toe-zah-mah)—Feudal lords who fought against the Tokugawa family and were generally mistrusted by the shogun.

tori-i (toe-ree-eh)—"Where the bird perches" in Japanese: a decorative gate.

Ukiyo-e (oo-key-oh-eh)—"Floating World": the name given to the highest expression of Japanese printmaking.

Waka (wah-kah)—Japanese stanzas linked with Chinese poems.

Yayoi (yah-oh-ee)—Culture in Japan during the neolithic period.

Yin and Yang (yin and yang)—The female and male (or positive and negative) principles that exist together in all things, according to many Chinese thinkers.

yoga (YO-gah)—The practice of "involvement without attachment" inherent in various Hindu religious activities.

zaibatsu (zay-eh-bah-soo)—A small group of families which has held extraordinary power in the financial activities of Japan.

APPENDIX D

A CHRONOLOGY OF ASIAN HISTORY

China	India	Japan	Southeast Asia	The West
B.C.	B.C.	B.C.	B.C.	B.C.
ca. 2205 Hsia Dynasty	ca. 4000 Indus cultures			ca. 3500 Egypt united
1766 Shang Dynasty	ca. 2500 Harappa falls			ca. 2750 Sargon I in Sumeria
ca. 1500 Eight Trigrams	ca. 2000 Aryan invasions			ca. 2750 Cuneiform used
ca. 1300 Supreme Being concept spreads	ca. 1600 Rig-Veda Classes develop			ca. 2169 Babylon founded
1122 Chou Dynasty	ca. 1500 Aryan-Dravidian Synthesis			ca. 2000 Stonehenge
1119 King Wu's empire	ca. 1200 Vedas, Brahmanas			ca. 2000 Cretan culture
ca. 1119 Central government	ca. 800 Upanishads			1800 Hammurabi's Code
Feudal landholding	ca. 567 Birth of Buddha	ca. 1000 Jomon Culture		ca. 1450 Mycenean Age
Civil service begins	ca. 500 Post-Vedic Period	ca. 660 Legendary origin		ca. 1200 Phonecian alphabet
604 Lao-tzu born	ca. 500 Jain Sect founded	ca. 500 Yayoi Culture		ca. 1000 Assyria rules
551 Confucius born	ca. 500 Buddhism			ca. 1000 Aryans move south
ca. 400 "100 Schools"	327 Alexander in India			ca. 950 Reign of Solomon
371 Mencius born	322 Chandragupta's victory			ca. 800 Carthage built
329 Chuang Tzu born	The Arthasastra		ca. 400 Indians arrive	776 First Olympiad
220 Highways built	273 Reign of Asoka		ca. 300 Bronze-Iron Age	753 Founding of Rome
206 Han Dynasty	270 Code of Manu		ca. 300 Buddhist missionaries	722 Iron in Assyria
ca. 206 Liu Pang's reign	ca. 232 Asoka dies			590 Roman Republic
Huns invade	185 Fall of Mauryas			539 Persian Empire
188 Liu's widow reigns				521 Darius I in Persia
180 Wen Ti emperor				490 Periclean Age
156 Ching Ti reigns				ca. 469 Socrates born
140 Reign of Wu Ti		260 Great Shrine of Ise		431 Peloponnesian War
Land distributed				323 Alexander dies
Military campaigns				323 Hellenistic Epoch
				ca. 264 First Punic War
				146 Carthage destroyed
				44 Caesar murdered
				27 Augustus: Pax Romana

A.D. 1–499

China	India	Southeast Asia	Japan	The West
ca. 9 Wang Mang's reign; Land distributed; State monopolies; Prices, taxes fixed ca. 22 "Red Eyebrows" 58 Han Ming Ti; Buddhism; Empire expanded 62 Pan Ch'ao's cavalry; Silk Road defended; Court conspiracies; "Yellow Turbans"; Gentry class; Sundials, clocks ca. 100 Paper invented ca. 175 Engravings 265 West Chin Dynasty; Barbarian invasions 317 East Chin Dynasty 386 North Wei Dynasty ca. 400 Sporadic warfare	ca. 50 Scythians invade ca. 150 Kushans invade; Kanishka reigns; Gandhara art; Buddhist schism ca. 250 Literature develops; Lawbooks; Mahabharata, Ramayana 320 Gupta Era begins 380 Chandragupta II reigns; Art, science flourish; Panchatantra; Mathematics develops; Hinduism emerges	ca. 50 Chinese in Tonkin ca. 100 Mon in lower Burma; Cult of Siva; Funan begins ca. 190 Champa founded ca. 400 Kaundinya rules Funan	ca. 400 Imperial Clan forms	29 Death of Christ 180 Marcus Aurelius dies; Decline of Rome 325 Council of Nicaea; Constantine aids Christianity 247 Goths cross Danube 277 Mani crucified 378 Battle of Adrianople 410 Alaric sacks Rome

500–999 A.D.

China	India	Southeast Asia	Japan	The West
575 Buddhism spreads 589 Sui Dynasty; Yang Ti's reign; Grand Canal; Great Wall repaired 612 Korea defeats China 618 Yang Ti murdered 618 T'ang Dynasty 626 Li Shih-min; Turkish invasions 640 Defeat of Turks; Land distributed; Ch'an Buddhism spreads; Arts flourish	540 Gupta Empire falls; Bhagavad-Puranas; "Four Ends of Man" 606 Harsha victorious	ca. 500 Cult of Vishnu ca. 539 Khmers in Funan ca. 600 Burmans arrive ca. 640 Sailendras on Java ca. 650 Thai migrations ca. 650 Sri Vijaya on Sumatra 670 Sri Vijayan envoys in China ca. 700 China trade increases 750 Burmans take Prome ca. 750 Buddhism on Java	552 Buddhists arrive; Soga clan is Buddhist; Civil wars; Shintoism vs. Buddhism 593 Buddhism made state religion 593 Buddhism is official 593 Envoys go to China 645 Soga clan in power 645 Taika Reforms 701 Taiho Codes	527 Justinian 622 Hejira of Mohammed 717 Battle of Constantinople

China	India	Southeast Asia	Japan	The West
713 Hsuan-tsung reigns	712 Arab invasions	ca. 785 Sailendra expands	710 Capital at Nara	732 Battle of Tours
755 An Lu-shan rebels		ca. 802 Jayavarman II: Angkor	Writing develops	800 Charlemagne
763 T'ang power high		ca. 850 Sailendra, Sri Vijaya unite	Confucianism, Buddhism	962 Otto crowned
845 Buddhists killed		ca. 898 Mataram established	Arts flourish	987 Hugh rules France
874 Hsi-tsung rules		ca. 980 Khmers invade Champa	794 Heian is capital	
874 Huang Ch'ao rebels		ca. 985 Mataram conquers Bali	ca. 800 Land ownership spreads	
889 Chu Wen			814 Minamoto clan begins	
890 Empire dissolves			889 Taira clan begins	
Commerce develops			995 Height of Fujiwara power	
Currency spreads				
Books distributed				
960 Sung Dynasty				
Reign of T'ai Tsu				
Confucianism aided				
Central government				
Hsi-hsia, Liao attack				

A.D. 1000–1499

China	India	Southeast Asia	Japan	The West
1069 Wang An-shih	ca. 1000 Mahmud's raids	1006 Sri Vijaya takes Mataram	1160 Taira clan in control	1016 Canute in England
Economic reforms		1025 Cholas raid Sri Vijaya	1183 Minamoto clan victorious	1054 Roman-Greek Orthodox schism
1100 Hiu-tsung reigns		1044 Burma expands	ca. 1186 Kamakura is capital	1066 Normans invade England
Arts flourish		1050 Mataram ends: Kadiri formed	1192 Yoritomo is shogun	1071 Seljuk Turks revive Islam
1127 Jurchen wars		1050 Khmers conquer Mon	Buddhism, arts flourish	1095 Crusades begin
1130 Chu Hsi born	ca. 1175 Ghori's invasions	1056 Anauratha is Buddhist	1205 Hojo Tokimasa regency	
Neo-Confucian Synthesis	1211 Delhi Sultanate	1057 Anauratha takes Thaton	1274 Mongols repulsed	
1215 Mongols in Peking		1177 Chams sack Angkor	1281 Mongols defeated	
1226 Jenghis Khan dies		1100 Sri Vijaya declines	1333 Go-Daigo attacks regency	
ca. 1260 Marco Polo in Asia		1180 Jayavarman VII Angkor rebuilt	1338 Ashikaga Takauji Two Courts	
1276 Kublai takes Hangchow		1190 Khmers rule Champa		
1279 Mongols seize South China		ca. 1190 Thais in north Burma		
1294 Kublai dies				
1356 Chu Yuan-chang succeeds	1398 Timur sacks Delhi			
1368 Chu destroys Karakorum	1498 Da Gama in Malabar			
Ming Dynasty				
1403 Reign of Yung-lo				

China	India	Japan	Southeast Asia	The West
			1200 Conversions to Islam	1215 Magna Carta
			1222 Singhasari subdues Kadiri	1274 St. Thomas dies / Middle Ages end
			1257 Mongols overrun Annam	1293 Roger Bacon dies
			1268 Kertanagara rules Java	
			1286 Kertanagara in Sumatra	
			1287 Mongols attack Pagan	
			1291 Kertanagara murdered	
			1293 Vijaya founds Majapahit	
		1368 Shogunate of Yoshimitsu / Height of Ashikaga	1300 Moslem conversions	1300 Renaissance
		1392 Imperial courts joined	1350 Majapahit Wars	1348 The Black Death
		1400 Feudalism elaborated	1350 Thais expand	1378 Christian schism
			1365 Majapahit rules islands	1400 Chaucer dies
1405 Cheng Ho			1395 Malacca founded	1452 Leonardo da Vinci born
ca. 1405 Early novels / Imperial City built / Trade with Europe			1400 Gujerati trade increases	1453 France wins 100 Years War / Turks capture Byzantium
ca. 1421 Nomadic invasions			1419 Siam attacks Malacca	1477 Polo's *Travels*
1432 Mings close China			1431 Annam independent	1492 Moslems lose Spain / Columbus's voyage
		ca. 1467 Ashikaga shogunate decays	1431 Thais seize Angkor	1486 Voyage of Diaz
			1489 Malacca defeats Siam	

A.D. 1500–1599

China	India	Japan	Southeast Asia	The West
ca. 1516 First Portuguese traders	ca. 1500 Delhi Sultanate collapses	1500 Sengoku Period / Feudal warfare	1509 D'Alburquerque is Viceroy / Portugal attacks Malacca	1517 Reformation
	1505 Portuguese in Goa	1542 Portuguese in Japan	1521 Magellan dies	1519 Magellan's voyage
	1524 Babur in India	1549 Francis Xavier arrives	1529 Portuguese in control	1529 Ottoman Turks defeated
	1526 Mogul Dynasty	1560 Oda Nobunaga		
	1556 Reign of Akbar / Central government			

China	India	Japan	Southeast Asia	The West
1557 Portuguese take Macao	High culture	1582 Oda Nobunaga dies 1582 Hideyoshi takes power 1587 Christians persecuted 1590 Korean expeditions 1590 Spaniards arrive 1592 Conflict in Korea 1598 Hideyoshi dies	1556 Burmans invade Siam 1564 Spanish in Philippines 1577 Franciscans in Philippines 1577 Drake in Moluccas 1597 Dutch attack Malacca	1530 Pizarro in Peru 1543 Copernicus 1558 Death of Charles V 1564 Birth of Shakespeare 1589 Henry IV: strife wanes

A.D. 1600–1699

China	India	Japan	Southeast Asia	The West
1601 Ricci in Peking 1622 Dutch attack Macao 1644 Last Ming ruler 1645 Manchus in Nanking 1662 K'ang-hsi regency Dual government created Campaigns: Tibet, Mongolia	1605 Reign of Jahangir 1609 English arrive 1627 Shah Jahan's reign Hindus persecuted Taj Mahal built 1659 Aurangzeb's reign New persecutions Rajput art ca. 1675 France wins trade	1603 Tokugawa shogunate (Edo) 1605 Reign of Ieyasu 1615 Hideyoshi-Tokugawa War 1616 Christians persecuted 1622 Iemitsu in control 1636 Spanish, English excluded 1637 Shimabara Rebellion 1639 Portuguese banished 1640 Japan closed to West 1641 Dutch confined	1620 French in Annam 1623 Dutch in Amboyna 1640 Dutch take Malacca ca. 1680 French trade in Siam 1687 Siamese massacre French	1608 Jamestown 1613 First Romanov Czar 1648 End of Thirty Years War 1649 English revolution 1661 Louis XIV 1688 England's Parliament supreme

A.D. 1700–1799

China	India	Japan	Southeast Asia	The West
1723 Missionaries banished 1736 Ch'ien-lung rules	ca. 1700 British open bases 1707 Downfall of Moguls 1739 Persians invade 1740 Mahrattas attack 1756 British-French War 1757 Battle of Plassy 1760 Sikhs seize Punjab 1761 Mahrattas retreat	ca. 1700 Bushido Code ca. 1780 Ukiyo-e, Kabuki	1740 Java rebels 1763 Spain regains Philippines 1790 British in Penang	1709 Russia takes power 1727 Death of Newton 1740 War of Austrian Succession 1765 End of Seven Years War 1776 Declaration of Independence

Timeline — The West · Southeast Asia · Japan · India · China

A.D. 1800–1899

The West
- 1789 French Revolution
- 1799 Bonaparte is First Consul
- 1815 Battle of Waterloo
- 1823 Monroe Doctrine
- 1825 First Railway
- 1830 Revolutions
- 1837 Victoria is queen
- 1848 *The Communist Manifesto*
- 1852 Napoleon III
- 1854 Crimean War
- 1858 *Origin of the Species*
- 1861 Civil War in U.S.
- 1861 Russian serfs freed
- 1866 Bismarck unifies Germany
- 1870 Franco-Prussian War
- 1898 Spanish-American War

Southeast Asia
- 1804 British in Dutch colonies
- 1819 Raffles buys Singapore
- ca. 1846 British in North Borneo
- ca. 1850 Siam "Westernizes"
- 1851 Burmans invade Malaya
- 1852 British take south Burma
- 1862 France seizes Cochin-China
- 1885 Britain annexes Burma
- 1887 France founds Indochina: Annam, Tonkin, Cambodia
- 1893 Laos added to Indochina
- 1898 Admiral Dewey at Manila Bay

Japan
- ca. 1800 Shinto Renaissance Provincial rebellions
- ca. 1850 Samurai titles sold
- 1853 Commodore Perry arrives
- 1854 Japanese–U.S. treaty
- 1856 U.S. consul arrives in Japan
- 1858 Civil war in Japan
- 1863 British shell Kagoshima
- 1867 Tokugawa shogun resigns
- 1868 Meiji Restoration
- 1869 Emperor regains power
- 1873 Reforms enacted Imperial Army created
- 1873 Christianity legalized
- 1877 Samurais rebel
- 1880 Zaibatsu gain power
- 1880 Liberal Party founded
- 1882 Kaishinto founded
- 1883 Ito visits Prussia
- 1889 New Constitution
- 1889 Ito made premier
- 1890 First general elections
- 1894 Japan invade Korea
- 1894 Sino-Japanese War

India
- 1763 British triumphant
- 1780 Mahrattas attack British
- 1804 Mahrattas defeated
- 1818 Gurkhas defeated
- 1844 Sikhs lose
- ca. 1850 India conquered
- 1857 Sepoy Rebellion
- 1858 British India Act Company replaced
- 1869 Birth of Gandhi
- 1877 Victoria becomes Empress
- 1885 National Congress

China
- ca. 1815 First British envoys
- 1829 Manchus ban opium
- 1839 Opium seized
- 1840 Britain declares war
- 1842 Treaty of Nanking
- 1842 British gain Hong Kong
- 1843 British gain ports
- 1850 T'ai-p'ing Rebellion starts
- 1856 British-French campaigns
- 1860 Allies enter Peking
- 1864 T'ai-p'ings defeated
- 1874 Japan in Ryukus, Formosa
- 1882 Japan attacks Korea
- 1894 Sino-Japanese War
- 1896 New concessions
- 1898 100 Days of Reform

A.D. 1900–

China

- 1900 Boxer Rebellion
- 1911 Chinese Revolution
- 1912 Chinese Republic
- 1912 Sun Yat-sen elected
- 1913 Yuan Shih-kai supreme
- 1915 21 Demands
- 1915 Nationalists at Nanking
- 1917 China joins Allies
- 1919 Allies reject China
- 1921 Communist Party formed
- 1924 Mongolian Republic
- 1924 "Three Principles"
- 1925 Sun Yat-sen dies
- 1928 Chiang attacks Communists
- 1931 "The Manchurian Incident"
- 1934 The Long March
- 1936 The Sian Incident
- 1937 Japan in China
- 1937 United Front
- 1942 Allies aid China
- 1943 Cairo Conference
- 1944 Communists advance
- 1945 Russia gains Outer Mongolia
- 1945 Nationalists in U.N.
- 1946 General Marshall's mission
- 1946 Civil war resumes
- 1948 Communists rout Chiang

India

- 1905 Bengal partitioned: riots
- 1906 Reform Act
- 1906 Moslem League founded
- 1909 Morley-Minto Reforms
- 1910 Terrorism
- 1915 Gandhi returns to India
- 1916 Tilak's leadership
- 1920 Satyagraha
- 1921 Gandhi rallies India
- 1935 Limited self-rule
- 1941 Nehru in power
- 1942 Civil disobedience
- 1943 "Quit India"
- 1943 Famine in Bengal
- 1944 Gandhi freed
- 1946 Hindu-Moslem strife
- 1947 India, Pakistan formed
- 1948 Gandhi assassinated
- 1951 First Five-Year Plan
- 1951 Ali Khan murdered
- 1952 Nehru is Prime Minister
- 1954 India's treaty with China
- 1955 Bandung Conference
- 1956 Pakistan's Constitution
- 1956 Second Five-Year Plan

Japan

- 1899 Extraterritoriality ends
- 1902 Treaty with Britain
- 1905 Treaty of Portsmouth
- 1910 Japan seizes Korea
- 1914 War on Germany
- 1917 German colonies annexed
- 1918 Rice riots
- 1920 More riots, strikes
- 1922 Parliament dissolves
- 1922 Communist Party founded
- 1922 Washington Peace Conference
- 1923 Great earthquake
- 1925 Peace Preservation Law
- 1927 Tanaka becomes premier
- 1928 Troops sent to Shantung
- 1930 London Naval Conference
- 1933 Japan seizes Manchuria
- 1933 Japan quits League of Nations
- 1936 Military coup
- 1937 Invasion of China
- 1940 Axis Pact
- 1940 Japan attacks Burma
- 1941 South Indochina seized
- 1941 Pearl Harbor

Southeast Asia

- 1902 U.S. annexes Philippines
- 1908 Indonesian nationalism
- 1918 Volksraad in Indonesia
- 1921 Burmese constitution
- 1934 Tydings-McDuffie Act
- 1935 Philippine Constitution
- 1935 Quezon elected
- 1935 British Burma Act
- 1937 Ba Maw, U Saw take power
- 1940 Japan, Siam sign treaty
- 1940 Siam invades Laos, Cambodia
- 1940 Japan takes Indochina
- 1941 Japan in Siam, Malaya, Burma, Dutch East Indies, Philippines
- 1942 Singapore falls
- 1942 Guerrillas in Vietnam
- 1942 Hukbalahaps (Philippines)
- 1945 Japanese withdraw
- 1946 Burma demands freedom

The West

- 1904 British-French alliance
- 1914 World War I
- 1917 Bolsheviks win
- 1920 Peace of Versailles
- 1920 League of Nations
- 1922 Mussolini
- 1928 Stalin's Five-Year Plan
- 1929 World Depression
- 1933 F. D. Roosevelt
- 1933 Hitler in Germany
- 1936 Spanish Civil War
- 1938 Munich Conference
- 1939 World War II
- 1940 Defeat of France
- 1945 Defeat of Germany
- 1945 Atomic energy
- 1945 U.N. founded

China	India	Japan	Southeast Asia	The West
1949 Chiang seizes Formosa	1956 V. Bhave	1942 Philippines conquered	1946 France regains Vietnam	1948 "Cold War" begins
1950 Landlords dispossessed	1961 India seizes Goa	1942 Japanese sea losses	1947 Elections in Burma	1950 Korean War begins
1951 China takes Tibet	1962 China invades India	1943 Guadalcanal	1947 Cambodian constitution	1952 Stalin dies
1951 "Volunteers" in Korea	1962 India mobilizes	1944 Southeast Asia defeats	1948 Collaborators executed	1957 Man-made satellites
1953 First Five-Year Plan	1963 Border disputes	1944 Premier Tojo resigns	1948 Vietnam divided	1960 European Common Market
1953 Korean armistice	1964 Nehru stricken	1945 Atomic bombs dropped	1949 French leave Laos	1963 President Kennedy dies
1954 Constitution		1945 Emperor seeks peace	1949 Karens revolt (Burma)	1964 Russia denounces China
1956 Free speech invited		1945 Surrender of Japan	1950 Indochina War	
1956 Strict controls resumed		1946 National elections	1951 Guerrilla warfare	
1957 Second Five-Year Plan		1946 Emperor disavows divinity	1954 French surrender	
1958 Communes begin		1947 New Constitution	1954 Cambodia is independent	
1959 Plagues widespread		1948 Land, education reforms	1954 SEATO	
1960 China aids nationalism		1950 Purge of Communists	1955 Jungle warfare	
1962 China invades India		1951 U.S.-Japanese Treaty	1959 Thailand coup	
1963 Sino-Russian strains		1952 End of occupation	1961 Truce in Laos	
1964 Diplomats tour Africa		1955 New parties formed	1963 Viet Cong gains	
1964 France recognizes China		1958 Production soars	1963 Malaysia formed	
		1960 Riots against U.S.	1964 Indonesia warns Malaysia	
		1962 Socialists gain	1964 Philippines progress	
		1963 Ikeda's re-election		
		1964 Striking economic gains		
		1964 Increasing China trade		

China	India	Japan	Southeast Asia	The West
1964 1st nuclear warhead exploded	1965 Clash with Pakistan	1971 Defense budget doubled	1966 Sukarno overthrown	1964 U.S. launches Gemini spacecraft
1965 Army ranks abolished	1967 Indira Gandhi Prime Minister	1972 Tanaka visits China	1966 U.S. bombs Hanoi	1964 Racial violence in U.S.
1965 Lin Piao foresees world revolution	1967 Clash with China	1973 Tanaka visits United States	1966 U.S. defoliates Vietnam jungles	1964 Johnson elected
1966 Cultural Revolution	1968 Alliance with Russia	1974 Critical inflation	1970 Sihanouk overthrown	1965 1st "walks" in space
1966 Red Guards riot	1969 Banks nationalized		1970 U.S. troops in Cambodia	1965 Peace demonstrations
1967 Cultural Revolution abates	1969 Communist victory in Bengal elections		1971 U.S. troops in Laos	1965 Watts riots
1969 Lin Piao named Mao's successor	1971 Army supports Bangladesh		1972 Martial law, Philippines	1966 U.S. student riots
1969 Border clash with Russians	1972 Bhutto leads Pakistan		1972 U.S. mines Haiphong harbor	1967 Israel wins "6-Day War"
1971 Lin Piao dies	1974 1st nuclear bomb		1973 U.S. bombs Hanoi	1967 "Black Power" movement
1971 Admitted to UN			1973 Armistice in Vietnam	1967 Anti-pollution movement
1972 Nixon's visit			1973 Armistice violations, Vietnam	1968 Martin Luther King dies
1972 Britain recognizes China			1974 War Spreads in Cambodia	1968 Russia invades Czechoslovakia
1973 Increasing world trade				1968 Nixon elected
				1969 My Lai charges
				1970 West German-Russian treaty
				1971 U.S. devalues dollar
				1972 Nixon visits China, Russia
				1972 Army limitation talks (SALT)
				1972 Britain joins Common Market
				1972 Peace negotiations
				1972 Nixon re-elected
				1973 Watergate investigation
				1973 Jupiter probe
				1973 4th Arab—Israeli war
				1973 Arab oil embargo
				1974 New energy sources explored

APPENDIX E

THE CONSTITUTION OF THE EMPIRE OF JAPAN

CHAPTER 1

THE EMPEROR

Article 1

The Empire of Japan shall be reigned over and governed by a line of Emperors unbroken for ages eternal.

Article 2

The Imperial Throne shall be succeeded to by Imperial male descendants, according to the provisions of the Imperial House Law.

Article 3

The Emperor is sacred and inviolable.

Article 4

The Emperor is the head of the Empire, combining in Himself the rights of sovereignty, and exercises them, according to the provisions of the present Constitution.

Article 5

The Emperor exercises the legislative power with the consent of the Imperial Diet.

Article 6

The Emperor gives sanction to laws, and orders them to be promulgated and executed.

Article 7

The Emperor convokes the Imperial Diet, opens, closes and prorogues it, and dissolves the House of Representatives.

Article 8

The Emperor, in consequence of an urgent necessity to maintain public safety or to avert public calamities, issues, when the Imperial Diet is not sitting, Imperial Ordinances in the place of law.

Such Imperial Ordinances are to be laid before the Imperial Diet at its next session, and when the Diet does not approve the said Ordinances, the Government shall declare them to be invalid for the future.

Article 9

The Emperor issues or causes to be issued, the Ordinances necessary for the carrying out of the laws, or for the maintenance of the public peace and order, and for the promotion of the welfare of the subjects. But no Ordinance shall in any way alter any of the existing laws.

Article 10

The Emperor determines the organization of the different branches of the administration, and salaries of all civil and military officers, and appoints and dismisses the same. Exceptions especially provided for in the present Constitution or in other laws, shall be in accordance with the respective provisions (bearing thereon).

Article 11

The Emperor has the supreme command of the Army and Navy.

Article 12

The Emperor determines the organization and peace standing of the Army and Navy.

Article 13

The Emperor declares war, makes peace, and concludes treaties.

Article 14

The Emperor declares a state of siege.
The conditions and effects of a state of siege shall be determined by law.

Article 15

The Emperor confers titles of nobility, rank, orders, and other marks of honor.

Article 16

The Emperor orders amnesty, pardon, commutation of punishments and rehabilitation.

Article 17

A Regency shall be instituted in conformity with the provisions of the Imperial House Law.
The Regent shall exercise the powers appertaining to the Emperor in His name.

Chapter 2

RIGHTS AND DUTIES OF SUBJECTS

Article 18

The conditions necessary for being a Japanese subject shall be determined by law.

Article 19

Japanese subjects may, according to qualifications determined in laws or ordinances, be appointed to civil or military or any other public offices equally.

Article 20

Japanese subjects are amenable to service in the Army or Navy, according to the provisions of law.

Article 21

Japanese subjects are amenable to the duty of paying taxes, according to the provisions of law.

Article 22

Japanese subjects shall have the liberty of abode and of changing the same within the limits of law.

Article 23

No Japanese subject shall be arrested, detained, tried or punished, unless according to law.

Article 24

No Japanese subject shall be deprived of his right of being tried by the judges determined by law.

Article 25

Except in cases provided for in the law, the house of no Japanese subject shall be entered or searched without his consent.

Article 26

Except in the cases mentioned in the law, the secrecy of the letters of every Japanese subject shall remain inviolate.

Article 27

The right of property of every Japanese subject shall remain inviolate.

Measures necessary to be taken for the public benefit shall be provided for by law.

Article 28

Japanese subjects shall, within limits not prejudicial to peace and order, and not antagonistic to their duties as subjects, enjoy freedom of religious belief.

Article 29

Japanese subjects shall, within the limits of law, enjoy the liberty of speech, writing, publication, public meetings and associations.

Article 30

Japanese subjects may present petitions, by observing the proper forms of respect, and by complying with the rules specially provided for the same.

Article 31

The provisions contained in the present Chapter shall not affect the exercise of the powers appertaining to the emperor, in times of war or in cases of a national emergency.

Article 32

Each and every one of the provisions contained in the preceding Articles of the present Chapter, that are not in conflict with the laws or the rules and discipline of the Army and Navy, shall apply to the officers and men of the Army and of the Navy.

CHAPTER 3

THE IMPERIAL DIET

Article 33

The Imperial Diet shall consist of two Houses, a House of Peers and a House of Representatives.

Article 34

The House of Peers shall, in accordance with the Ordinance concerning the House of Peers, be composed of the members of the Imperial Family, of the orders of nobility, and of those persons, who have been nominated thereto by the Emperor.

Article 35

The House of Representatives shall be composed of Members

elected by the people, according to the provisions of the Law of Election.

Article 36

No one can at one and the same time be a Member of both Houses.

Article 37

Every law requires the consent of the Imperial Diet.

Article 38

Both Houses shall vote upon projects of law submitted to it by the Government, and may respectively initiate projects of law.

Article 39

A Bill, which has been rejected by either the one or the other of the two Houses, shall not be again brought in during the same session.

Article 40

Both Houses can make representations to the Government, as to laws or upon any other subject. When, however, such representations are not accepted, they cannot be made a second time during the same session.

Article 41

The Imperial Diet shall be convoked every year.

Article 42

A session of the Imperial Diet shall last during three months. In case of necessity, the duration of a session may be prolonged by Imperial Order.

Article 43

When urgent necessity arises, an extraordinary session may be convoked, in addition to the ordinary one.

The duration of an extraordinary session shall be determined by Imperial Order.

Article 44

The opening, closing, prolongation of session, and prorogation of the Imperial Diet, shall be effected simultaneously for both Houses.

In case the House of Representatives has been ordered to dissolve, the House of Peers shall at the same time be prorogued.

Article 45

When the House of Representatives has been ordered to dissolve. Members shall be caused by Imperial Order to be newly elected, and the new House shall be convoked within five months from the day of dissolution.

Article 46

No debate can be opened and no vote can be taken in either House of the Imperial Diet, unless not less than one third of the whole number of the Members thereof is present.

Article 47

Votes shall be taken in both Houses by absolute majority. In the case of a tie vote the President shall have the deciding vote.

Article 48

The deliberations of either House shall be public. The deliberations may, upon demand of the Government or by resolution of the House, be held in secret sitting.

Article 49

Both Houses of the Imperial Diet may respectively present addresses to the Emperor.

Article 50

Both Houses may receive petitions presented by subjects.

Article 51

Both Houses may enact, besides what is provided for in the present Constitution and in the Law of the Houses, rules necessary for the management of their internal affairs.

Article 52

No Member of either House shall be held responsible outside the respective Houses, for any opinion uttered or for any vote given in the House. When, however, a Member himself has given publicity to his opinions by public speech, by documents in print or in writing, or by any similar means, he shall, in the matter, be amenable to the general law.

Article 53

The Members of both Houses shall, during the session, be free from arrest, unless with the consent of the House, except in cases of flagrant delicts, or of offenses connected with a state of internal commotion or with a foreign trouble.

Article 54

The Ministers of State and the Delegates of the Government may, at any time, take seats and speak in either House.

CHAPTER 4

THE MINISTERS OF STATE AND THE PRIVY COUNCIL

Article 55

The respective Ministers of State shall give their advice to the Emperor, and be responsible for it.

All Laws, Imperial Ordinances and Imperial Rescripts of whatever kind, that relate to the affairs of the State, require the countersignature of a Minister of State.

Article 56

The Privy Councillors shall, in accordance with the provisions for the organization of the Privy Council, deliberate upon important matters of State, when they have been consulted by the Emperor.

CHAPTER 5

THE JUDICATURE

Article 57

The Judicature shall be exercised by the Courts of Law according to law, in the name of the Emperor.

The organization of the Courts of Law shall be determined by law.

Article 58

The judges shall be appointed from among those, who possess proper qualifications according to law.

No judge shall be deprived of his position, unless by way of criminal sentence or disciplinary punishment.

Rules for disciplinary punishment shall be determined by law.

Article 59

Trials and judgments of a Court shall be conducted publicly. When, however, there exists any fear, that such publicity may be prejudicial to peace and order, or to the maintenance of public morality, the public trial may be suspended by provision of law or by the decision of the Court of Law.

Article 60

All matters, that fall within the competency of a special Court, shall be specially provided for by law.

Article 61

No suit at law, which relates to right alleged to have been infringed by the illegal measures of the administrative authorities, and which shall come within the competency of the Court of Administrative Litigation specially established by law, shall be taken cognizance of by a Court of Law.

CHAPTER 6

FINANCE

Article 62

The imposition of a new tax or the modification of the rates (of an existing one) shall be determined by law.

However, all such administrative fees or other revenue having the nature of compensation shall not fall within the category of the above clause.

The raising of national loans and the contracting of other liabilities to the charge of the National Treasury, except those that are provided in the Budget, shall require the consent of the Imperial Diet.

Article 63

The taxes levied at present shall, in so far as they are not remodelled by a new law, be collected according to the old system.

Article 64

The expenditure and revenue of the State require the consent of the Imperial Diet by means of the annual Budget.

Any and all expenditures overpassing the appropriations set forth in the Titles and Paragraphs of the Budget, or that are not provided for in the Budget, shall subsequently require the approbation of the Imperial Diet.

Article 65

The Budget shall be first laid before the House of Representatives.

Article 66

The expenditures of the Imperial House shall be defrayed every year out of the National Treasury, according to the present fixed amount for the same, and shall not require the consent thereto of the Imperial Diet, except in case an increase thereof is found necessary.

155

Article 67

Those already fixed expenditures based by the Constitution upon the powers appertaining to the Emperor, and such expenditures as may have arisen by the effect of law, or that appertain to the legal obligations of the Government, shall be neither rejected nor reduced by the Imperial Diet, without the concurrence of the Government.

Article 68

In order to meet special requirements, the Government may ask the consent of the Imperial Diet to a certain amount as a Continuing Expenditure Fund, for a previously fixed number of years.

Article 69

In order to supply deficiencies which are unavoidable in the Budget, and to meet requirements unprovided for in the same, a Reserve Fund shall be provided in the Budget.

Article 70

When the Imperial Diet cannot be convoked, owing to the external or internal condition of the country, in case of urgent need for the maintenance of public safety, the Government may take all necessary financial measures, by means of an Imperial Ordinance.

In the case mentioned in the preceding clause, the matter shall be submitted to the Imperial Diet at its next session, and its approbation shall be obtained thereto.

Article 71

When the Imperial Diet has not voted on the Budget, or when the Budget has not been brought into actual existence, the Government shall carry out the Budget of the preceding year.

Article 72

The final account of the expenditures and revenue of the State shall be verified and confirmed by the Board of Audit, and it shall be submitted by the Government to the Imperial Diet, together with the report of verification of the said Board.

The organization and competency of the Board of Audit shall be determined by law separately.

CHAPTER 7

SUPPLEMENTARY RULES

Article 73

When it has become necessary in future to amend the provisions of the present Constitution, a project to that effect shall be submitted to the Imperial Diet by Imperial Order.

In the above case, either House can open the debate, unless not less than two-thirds of the whole number of Members are present, and no amendment can be passed, unless a majority of not less than two-thirds of the Members present is obtained.

Article 74

No modification of the Imperial House Law shall be required to be submitted to the deliberation of the Imperial Diet.

No provision of the present Constitution can be modified by the Imperial House Law.

Article 75

No modification can be introduced into the Constitution, or into the Imperial House Law, during the time of a Regency.

Article 76

Existing legal enactments, such as laws, regulations, Ordinances, or by whatever names they may be called, shall, so far as they do not conflict with the present Constitution, continue in force.

All existing contracts or orders, that entail obligations upon the Governments, and that are connected with expenditure, shall come within the scope of Art. 67.

APPENDIX F

THE IMPERIAL RESCRIPT RENOUNCING DIVINITY

In greeting the New Year, we recall to mind that the Emperor Meiji proclaimed as the basis of our national policy the five clauses of the Charter at the beginning of the Meiji era. The Charter oath signified:

(1) Deliberative assemblies shall be established and all measures of government decided in accordance with public opinion.

(2) All classes, high and low, shall unite in vigorously carrying on the affairs of state.

(3) All common people, no less than the civil and military officials, shall be allowed to fulfill their just desires so that there may not be any discontent among them.

(4) All the observed usages of the old shall be broken through and the equity and justice to be found in the workings of nature shall serve as the basis of action.

(5) Wisdom and knowledge shall be sought throughout the world for the purpose of promoting the welfare of the empire.

The proclamation is evident in its significance and high in its ideals. We wish to make this oath anew and restore the country to stand on its own feet again. We have to affirm the principles embodied in the Charter and proceed unflinchingly toward elimination of misguided practices of the past; and, keeping in close touch with the desires of the people, we will construct a new Japan, through thoroughly being pacific, the officials and people alike obtaining rich culture and advancing the standard of living of the people.

The devastation of the war inflicted upon our cities, the miseries of the destitute, the stagnation of trade, shortage of food and the great and growing number of the unemployed are indeed heartrending, but if the nation is firmly united in its resolve to face the present ordeal and to see civilization consistently in peace, a bright future will undoubtedly be ours, not only for our country but for the whole of humanity.

Love of the family and love of country are especially strong in this country. With more of this devotion should we not work toward love of mankind.

We feel deeply concerned to note that consequent upon the protracted war ending in our defeat, our people are liable to grow restless and to fall into the slough of despond. Radical tendencies in excess are gradually spreading and the sense of morality tends to lose its hold on the people, with the result that there are signs of confusion of thoughts.

We stand by the people and we wish always to share with them in their moment of joys and sorrows. The ties between us and our people have always stood upon mutual trust and affection. They do not depend upon mere legends and myths. They are not predicated on the false conception that the emperor is divine and that the Japanese people are superior to other races and fated to rule the world.

Our government should make every effort to alleviate their trials and tribulations. At the same time, we trust that the people will rise to the occasion and will strive courageously for the solution of their outstanding difficulties and for the development of industry and culture. Acting upon a consciousness of solidarity and mutual aid and broad tolerance in their civic life, they will prove themselves worthy of their best tradition. By their supreme endeavors in that direction they will be able to render their substantial contribution to the welfare and advancement of mankind.

The resolution for the year should be made at the beginning of the year. We expect our people to join us in all exertions looking to accomplishment of this great undertaking with an indominable spirit.

158

APPENDIX G

STATEMENT BY GENERAL DOUGLAS MACARTHUR

TO THE PEOPLE OF JAPAN:

A New Year has come. With it a new day dawns for Japan. No longer is the future to be settled by a few. The shackles of militarism, of feudalism, of regimentation, of body and soul have been removed. Thought control and the abuse of education are no more. All now enjoy religious freedom and the right of speech without undue restraint. Free assembly is guaranteed.

The removal of this national enslavement means freedom for the people, but at the same time it imposes upon them the individual duty to think and to act each on his own initiative. It is necessary for the masses of Japan to awaken to the fact that they now have the power to govern and what is done must be done by themselves.

It is my hope that the New Year may be the beginning for them of "the way and the truth and the light."

January 1, 1946

APPENDIX H

THE CONSTITUTION OF JAPAN

We, the Japanese people, acting through our duly elected representatives in the National Diet, determined that we shall secure for ourselves and our posterity the fruits of peaceful cooperation with all nations and the blessings of liberty throughout this land, and resolved that never again shall we be visited with the horrors of war through the action of government, do proclaim that sovereign power resides with the people and do firmly establish this Constitution. Government is a sacred trust of the people, the authority for which is derived from the people, the powers of which are exercised by the representatives of the people, and the benefits of which are enjoyed by the people. This is a universal principle of mankind upon which this Constitution is founded. We reject and revoke all constitutions, laws, ordinances and rescripts in conflict herewith.

We, the Japanese people, desire peace for all time and are deeply conscious of the high ideals controlling human relationship, and we have determined to preserve our security and existence, trusting in the justice and faith of the peace-loving peoples of the world. We desire to occupy an honoured place in an international society striving for the preservation of peace, and the banishment of tyranny and slavery, oppression and intolerance for all time from the earth. We recognize that all peoples of the world have the right to live in peace, free from fear and want.

We believe that no nation is responsible to itself alone, but that laws of political morality are universal; and that obedience to such laws is incumbent upon all nations who would sustain their own sovereignty and justify their sovereign relationship with other nations.

We, the Japanese people, pledge our national honor to accomplish these high ideals and purposes with all our resources.

CHAPTER 1

THE EMPEROR

Article 1

The Emperor shall be the symbol of the State and of the unity of the people, deriving his position from the will of the people with whom resides sovereign power.

Article 2

The Imperial Throne shall be dynastic and succeeded to in accordance with the Imperial House Law passed by the Diet.

Article 3

The advice and approval of the Cabinet shall be required for all acts of the Emperor in matters of state, and the Cabinet shall be responsible therefor.

Article 4

The Emperor shall perform only such acts in matters of state as are provided for in this Constitution and he shall not have powers related to government.

The Emperor may delegate the performance of his acts in matters of state as may be provided by law.

Article 5

When, in accordance with the Imperial House Law, a Regency is established, the Regent shall perform his acts in matters of state in the

Emperor's name. In this case, paragraph one of the preceding article will be applicable.

Article 6

The Emperor shall appoint the Prime Minister as designated by the Diet.

The Emperor shall appoint the Chief Judge of the Supreme Court as designated by the Cabinet.

Article 7

The Emperor, with the advice and approval of the Cabinet, shall perform the following acts in matters of state on behalf of the people:

Promulgation of amendments of the constitution, laws, cabinet orders and treaties.

Convocation of the Diet.

Dissolution of the House of Representatives.

Proclamation of general election of members of the Diet.

Attestation of the appointment and dismissal of Ministers of State and other officials as provided for by law, and of full powers and credentials of Ambassadors and Ministers.

Attestation of general and special amnesty, commutation of punishment, reprieve, and restoration of rights.

Awarding of honours.

Attestation of instruments of ratification and other diplomatic documents as provided for by law.

Receiving foreign ambassadors and ministers.

Performance of ceremonial functions.

Article 8

No property can be given to, or received by, the Imperial House, nor can any gifts be made therefrom, without the authorization of the Diet.

Chapter 2

RENUNCIATION OF WAR

Article 9

Aspiring sincerely to an international peace based on justice and order, the Japanese people forever renounce war as a sovereign right of the nation and the threat or use of force as means of settling international disputes.

In order to accomplish the aim of the preceding paragraph, land, sea, and air forces, as well as other war potential, will never be maintained. The right of belligerency of the state will not be recognized.

CHAPTER 3

RIGHTS AND DUTIES OF THE PEOPLE

Article 10

The conditions necessary for being a Japanese national shall be determined by law.

Article 11

The people shall not be prevented from enjoying any of the fundamental human rights. These fundamental human rights guaranteed to the people by this Constitution shall be conferred upon the people of this and future generations as eternal and inviolate rights.

Article 12

The freedom and rights guaranteed to the people by this Constitution shall be maintained by the constant endeavour of the people, who shall refrain from any abuse of these freedoms and rights and shall always be responsible for utilizing them for the public welfare.

Article 13

All of the people shall be respected as individuals. Their right to life, liberty, and the pursuit of happiness shall, to the extent that it does not interfere with the public welfare, be the supreme consideration in legislation and in other governmental affairs.

Article 14

All of the people are equal under the law and there shall be no discrimination in political, economic or social relations because of race, creed, sex, social status or family origin.

Peers and peerage shall not be recognized.

No privilege shall accompany any award of honour, decoration or any distinction, nor shall any such award be valid beyond the lifetime of the individual who now holds or hereafter may receive it.

Article 15

The people have the inalienable right to choose their public officials and to dismiss them.

All public officials are servants of the whole community and not of any group thereof.

Universal adult suffrage is guaranteed with regard to the election of public officials.

In all elections, secrecy of the ballot shall not be violated. A voter shall not be answerable, publicly or privately, for the choice he has made.

Article 16

Every person shall have the right of peaceful petition for the redress of damage, for the removal of public officials, for the enactment, repeal or amendment of laws, ordinances or regulations and for other matters, nor shall any person be in any way discriminated against for sponsoring such a petition.

Article 17

Every person may sue for redress as provided by law from the State or public entity, in case he has suffered damage through illegal act of any public official.

Article 18

No person shall be held in bondage of any kind. Involuntary servitude, except as punishment for crime, is prohibited.

Article 19

Freedom of thought and conscience shall not be violated.

Article 20

Freedom of religion is guaranteed to all. No religious organization shall receive any privileges from the State, nor exercise any political authority.

No person shall be compelled to take part in any religious act, celebration, rite or practice.

The State and its organs shall refrain from religious education or any other religious activity.

Article 21

Freedom of assembly and association as well as speech, press and all other forms of expression are guaranteed.

No censorship shall be maintained, nor shall the secrecy of any means of communication be violated.

Article 22

Every person shall have freedom to choose and change his residence and to choose his occupation to the extent that it does not interfere with the public welfare.

Freedom of all persons to move to a foreign country and to divest themselves of their nationality shall be inviolate.

Article 23

Academic freedom is guaranteed.

Article 24

Marriage shall be based only on the mutual consent of both sexes and it shall be maintained through mutual co-operation with the equal rights of husband and wife as a basis.

With regard to choice of spouse, property rights, inheritance, choice of domicile, divorce and other matters pertaining to marriage and the family, laws shall be enacted from the standpoint of individual dignity and the essential equality of the sexes.

Article 25

All people shall have the right to maintain the minimum standards of wholesome and cultured living.

In all spheres of life, the State shall use its endeavours for the promotion and extension of social welfare and security, and of public health.

Article 26

All people shall have the right to receive an equal education correspondent to their ability, as provided by law.

All people shall be obligated to have all boys and girls under their protection receive ordinary education as provided for by law. Such compulsory education shall be free.

Article 27

All people shall have the right and the obligation to work.

Standards for wages, hours, rest and other working conditions shall be fixed by law.

Children shall not be exploited.

Article 28

The right of workers to organize and to bargain and act collectively is guaranteed.

Article 29

The right to own or to hold property is inviolable.

Property rights shall be defined by law, in conformity with the public welfare.

Private property may be taken for public use upon just compensation therefor.

Article 30

The people shall be liable to taxation as provided by law.

Article 31

No person shall be deprived of life or liberty, nor shall any other criminal penalty be imposed, except according to procedure established by law.

Article 32

No person shall be denied the right of access to the courts.

Article 33

No person shall be apprehended except upon warrant issued by a competent judicial officer which specifies the offense with which the person is charged, unless he is apprehended, the offense being committed.

Article 34

No person shall be arrested or detained without being at once informed of the charges against him or without the immediate privilege of counsel; nor shall he be detained without adequate cause; and upon demand of any person such cause must be immediately shown in open court in his presence and the presence of his counsel.

Article 35

The right of all persons to be secure in their homes, papers and effects against entries, searches and seizures shall not be impaired except upon warrant issued for adequate cause and particularly describing the place to be searched and things to be seized, or except as provided by Article 33.

Each search or seizure shall be made upon separate warrant issued by a competent judicial officer.

Article 36

The infliction of torture by any public officer and cruel punishments are absolutely forbidden.

Article 37

In all criminal cases the accused shall enjoy the right to a speedy and public trial by an impartial tribunal.

He shall be permitted full opportunity to examine all witnesses, and he shall have the right of compulsory process for obtaining witnesses on his behalf at public expense.

At all times the accused shall have the assistance of competent counsel who shall, if the accused is unable to secure the same by his own efforts, be assigned to his use by the State.

Article 38

No person shall be compelled to testify against himself.

Confession made under compulsion, torture or threat, or after prolonged arrest or detention shall not be admitted in evidence.

No person shall be convicted or punished in cases where the only proof against him is his own confession.

Article 39

No person shall be held criminally liable for an act which was lawful at the time it was committed, or of which he has been acquitted, nor shall he be placed in double jeopardy.

Article 40

Any person, in case he is acquitted after he has been arrested or detained, may sue the State for redress as provided by law.

CHAPTER 4

THE DIET

Article 41

The Diet shall be the highest organ of state power, and shall be the sole law-making organ of the State.

Article 42

The Diet shall consist of two Houses, namely the House of Representatives and the House of Councillors.

Article 43

Both Houses shall consist of elected members, representatives of the people.

The number of the members of each House shall be fixed by law.

Article 44

The qualifications of members of both Houses and their electors shall be fixed by law. However, there shall be no discrimination because of race, creed, sex, social status, family origin, education, property or income.

Article 45

The term of office of members of the House of Representatives shall be four years. However, the term shall be terminated before the full term is up in case the House of Representatives is dissolved.

Article 46

The term of office of members of the House of Councillors shall be six years, and election for half the members shall take place every three years.

Article 47

Electoral districts, method of voting and other matters pertaining to the method of election of members of both Houses shall be fixed by law.

Article 48

No person shall be permitted to be a member of both Houses simultaneously.

Article 49

Members of both Houses shall receive appropriate annual payment from the national treasury in accordance with law.

Article 50

Except in cases provided by law, members of both Houses shall be exempt from apprehension while the Diet is in session, and any members apprehended before the opening of the session shall be freed during the term of the session upon demand of the House.

Article 51

Members of both Houses shall not be held liable outside the House for speeches, debates or votes cast inside the House.

Article 52

An ordinary session of the Diet shall be convoked once per year.

Article 53

The Cabinet may determine to convoke extraordinary sessions of the Diet. When a quarter or more of the total members of either House makes the demand, the Cabinet must determine on such convocation.

Article 54

When the House of Representatives is dissolved, there must be a general election of members of the House of Representatives within forty (40) days from the date of dissolution, and the Diet must be convoked within thirty (30) days from the date of the election.

When the House of Representatives is dissolved, the House of Councillors is closed at the same time. However, the Cabinet may in time of national emergency convoke the House of Councillors in emergency session.

Measures taken at such session as mentioned in the proviso of the preceding paragraph shall be provisional and shall become null and void unless agreed to by the House of Representatives within a period of ten (10) days after the opening of the next session of the Diet.

Article 55

Each House shall judge disputes related to qualifications of its members. However, in order to deny a seat to any member, it is necessary to pass a resolution by a majority of two-thirds or more of the members present.

Article 56

Business cannot be transacted in either House unless one-third or more of total membership is present.

All matters shall be decided, in each House, by a majority of those present, except as elsewhere provided in the Constitution, and in case of a tie, the presiding officer shall decide the issue.

Article 57

Deliberation in each House shall be public. However, a secret meeting may be held where a majority of two-thirds or more of those members present passes a resolution therefor.

Each House shall keep a record of proceedings. This record shall be published and given general circulation, excepting such parts of proceedings of secret session as may be deemed to require secrecy.

Upon demand of one-fifth or more of the members present, votes of the members on any matter shall be recorded in the minutes.

Article 58

Each House shall select its own president and other officials.

Each House shall establish its rules pertaining to meetings, proceedings and internal discipline, and may punish members for disorderly conduct. However, in order to expel a member, a majority of two-thirds or more of those members present must pass a resolution thereon.

Article 59

A bill becomes a law on passage by both Houses, except as otherwise provided by the Constitution.

A bill which is passed by the House of Representatives, and upon which the House of Councillors makes a decision different from that of the House of Representatives, becomes a law when passed a second time by the House of Representatives by a majority of two-thirds or more of the members present.

The provision of the preceding paragraph does not preclude the House of Representatives from calling for the meeting of a joint committee of both Houses, provided for by law.

Failure by the House of Councillors to take final action within sixty (60) days after receipt of a bill passed by the House of Representatives, time in recess excepted, may be determined by the House of Representatives to constitute a rejection of the said bill by the House of Councillors.

Article 60

The budget must first be submitted to the House of Representatives.

Upon consideration of the budget, when the House of Councillors makes a decision different from that of the House of Representatives, and when no agreement can be reached even through a joint committee of both Houses, provided for by law, or in the case of failure by the House of Councillors to take final action within thirty (30) days, the period of recess excluded, after the receipt of the budget passed by the House of Representatives, the decision of the House of Representatives shall be the decision of the Diet.

Article 61

The second paragraph of the preceding article applies also to the Diet approval required for the conclusion of treaties.

Article 62

Each House may conduct investigations in relation to government, and may demand the presence and testimony of witnesses, and the production of records.

Article 63

The Prime Minister and other Ministers of State may, at any time, appear in either House for the purpose of speaking on bills, regardless of whether they are members of the House or not. They must appear when their presence is required in order to give answers or explanations.

Article 64

The Diet shall set up an impeachment court from among the members of both Houses for the purpose of trying those judges against whom removal proceedings have been instituted.

Matters relating to impeachment shall be provided by law.

CHAPTER 5

THE CABINET

Article 65

Executive power shall be vested in the Cabinet.

Article 66

The Cabinet shall consist of the Prime Minister, who shall be its head, and other Ministers of State, as provided for by law.

The Prime Minister and other Ministers of State must be civilians.

The Cabinet, in the exercise of executive power, shall be collectively responsible to the Diet.

Article 67

The Prime Minister shall be designated from among the members of the Diet by a resolution of the Diet. This designation shall precede all other business.

If the House of Representatives and the House of Councillors disagree and if no agreement can be reached even through a joint committee of both Houses, provided for by law, or the House of Councillors fails to make designation within ten (10) days, exclusive of the period of recess, after the House of Representatives has made designation, the decision of the House of Representatives shall be the decision of the Diet.

Article 68

The Prime Minister shall appoint the Ministers of State. However, a majority of their number must be chosen from among the members of the Diet.

The Prime Minister may remove the Ministers of State as he chooses.

Article 69

If the House of Representatives passes a non-confidence resolution, or rejects a confidence resolution, the Cabinet shall resign en masse, unless the House of Representatives is dissolved within ten (10) days.

Article 70

When there is a vacancy in the post of Prime Minister, or upon the first convocation of the Diet after a general election of members of the House of Representatives, the Cabinet shall resign en masse.

Article 71

In cases mentioned in the two preceding articles, the Cabinet shall continue its functions until the time when a new Prime Minister is appointed.

Article 72

The Prime Minister, representing the Cabinet, submits bills, reports on general national affairs and foreign relations to the Diet and exercises control and supervision over various administrative branches.

Article 73

The Cabinet, in addition to other general administrative functions, shall perform the following functions:

Administer the law faithfully; conduct affairs of state.

Manage foreign affairs.

Conclude treaties. However, it shall obtain prior or, depending on circumstances, subsequent approval of the Diet.

Administer the civil service, in accordance with standards established by law.

Prepare the budget, and present it to the Diet.

Enact cabinet orders in order to execute the provisions of this Constitution and of the law.

However, it cannot include penal provisions in such cabinet orders unless authorized by such law.

Decide on general amnesty, special amnesty, commutation of punishment, reprieve, and restoration of rights.

Article 74

All laws and cabinet orders shall be signed by the competent Minister of State and countersigned by the Prime Minister.

Article 75

The Ministers of State, during their tenure of office, shall not be subject to legal action without the consent of the Prime Minister. However, the right to take that action is not impaired hereby.

CHAPTER 6

JUDICIARY

Article 76

The whole judicial power is vested in a Supreme Court and in such inferior courts as are established by law.

No extraordinary tribunal shall be established, nor shall any organ or agency of the Executive be given final judicial power.

All judges shall be independent in the exercise of their conscience and shall be bound only by this Constitution and the laws.

Article 77

The Supreme Court is vested with the rule-making power under which it determines the rules of procedure and of practice, and of matters relating to attorneys, the internal discipline of the courts and the administration of judicial affairs.

Public procurators shall be subject to the rule-making power of the Supreme Court.

The Supreme Court may delegate the power to make rules for inferior courts to such courts.

Article 78

Judges shall not be removed except by public impeachment unless judicially declared mentally or physically incompetent to perform official duties. No disciplinary action against judges shall be administered by any executive organ or agency.

Article 79

The Supreme Court shall consist of a Chief Judge and such number of judges as may be determined by law; all such judges excepting the Chief Judge shall be appointed by the Cabinet.

The appointment of the judges of the Supreme Court shall be reviewed by the people at the first general election of members of the House of Representatives following their appointment, and shall be reviewed again at the first general election of members of the House of Representatives after a lapse of ten (10) years, and in the same manner thereafter.

In cases mentioned in the foregoing paragraph, when the majority of the voters favors the dismissal of a judge, he shall be dismissed.

Matters pertaining to review shall be prescribed by law.

The judges of the Supreme Court shall be retired upon the attainment of the age as fixed by law.

All such judges shall receive, at regular stated intervals, adequate compensation which shall not be decreased during their terms of office.

Article 80

The judges of the inferior courts shall be appointed by the Cabinet from a list of persons nominated by the Supreme Court. All such judges shall hold office for a term of ten (10) years with privilege of reappointment, provided that they shall be retired upon the attainment of the age as fixed by law.

The judges of the inferior courts shall receive, at regular stated intervals, adequate compensation which shall not be decreased during their terms of office.

Article 81

The Supreme Court is the court of last resort with power to determine the constitutionality of any law, order, regulation or official act.

Article 82

Trials shall be conducted and judgment declared publicly. Where a court unanimously determines publicity to be dangerous to public order or morals, a trial may be conducted privately, but trials of political offenses, offenses involving the press or cases wherein the right of people as guaranteed in Chapter 3 of this Constitution are in question shall always be conducted publicly.

CHAPTER 7

FINANCE

Article 83

The power to administer national finances shall be exercised as the Diet shall determine.

Article 84

No new taxes shall be imposed or existing ones modified except by law or under such conditions as law may prescribe.

Article 85

No money shall be expended, nor shall the State obligate itself, except as authorized by the Diet.

Article 86

The Cabinet shall prepare and submit to the Diet for its consideration and decision a budget for each fiscal year.

Article 87

In order to provide for unforeseen deficiencies in the budget, a reserve fund may be authorized by the Diet to be expended upon the responsibility of the Cabinet.

The Cabinet must get subsequent approval of the Diet for all payments from the reserve fund.

Article 88

All property of the Imperial Household shall belong to the State.

All expenses of the Imperial Household shall be appropriated by the Diet in the budget.

Article 89

No public money or other property shall be expended or appropriated for the use, benefit or maintenance of any religious institution or association, or for any charitable, educational or benevolent enterprises not under the control of public authority.

Article 90

Final accounts of the expenditures and revenues of the State shall be audited annually by a Board of Audit and submitted by the Cabinet to the Diet, together with the statement of audit during the fiscal year immediately following the period covered.

The organization and competency of the Board of Audit shall be determined by law.

Article 91

At regular intervals and at least annually the Cabinet shall report to the Diet and the people on the state of national finances.

CHAPTER 8

LOCAL SELF-GOVERNMENT

Article 92

Regulations concerning organization and operations of local public entities shall be fixed by law in accordance with the principle of local autonomy.

Article 93

The local public entities shall establish assemblies as their deliberative organs, in accordance with law.

The chief executive officers of all local public entities, the members of their assemblies, and such other local officials as may be determined by law shall be elected by direct popular vote within their several communities.

Article 94

Local public entities shall have the right to manage their property, affairs and administration and to enact their own regulations within law.

Article 95

A special law applicable only to one local public entity cannot be enacted by the Diet without the consent of the majority of the voters of the local public entity concerned, obtained in accordance with law.

CHAPTER 9

AMENDMENTS

Article 96

Amendments to this Constitution shall be initiated by the Diet, through a concurring vote of two-thirds or more of all the members of each House and shall thereupon be submitted to the people for ratification, which shall require the affirmative vote of a majority of all votes cast thereon, at a special referendum or at such election as the Diet shall specify.

Amendments when so ratified shall immediately be promulgated by the Emperor in the name of the people, as an integral part of this Constitution.

CHAPTER 10

SUPREME LAW

Article 97

The fundamental human rights by this Constitution guaranteed to the people of Japan are fruits of the age-old struggle of man to be free; they have survived the many exacting tests for durability and are conferred upon this and future generations in trust, to be held for all time inviolate.

Article 98

This Constitution shall be the supreme law of the nation and no law, ordinance, imperial rescript or other act of government, or part thereof, contrary to the provisions hereof, shall have legal force or validity.

The treaties concluded by Japan and established laws of nations shall be faithfully observed.

Article 99

The Emperor or the Regent as well as Ministers of State, members of the Diet, judges, and all other public officials have the obligation to respect and uphold this Constitution.

CHAPTER 11

SUPPLEMENTARY PROVISIONS

Article 100

This Constitution shall be enforced as from the day when the period of six months will have elapsed counting from the day of its promulgation.

The enactment of laws necessary for the enforcement of this Constitution, the election of members of the House of Councillors, and the procedure for the convocation of the Diet and other preparatory procedures necessary for the enforcement of this Constitution, may be executed before the day prescribed in the preceding paragraph.

Article 101

If the House of Councillors is not constituted before the effective date of this Constitution, the House of Representatives shall function as the Diet until such time as the House of Councillors shall be constituted.

Article 102

The term of office for half the members of the House of Councillors serving in the first term under this Constitution shall be three years. Members falling under this category shall be determined in accordance with law.

Article 103

The Ministers of State, members of the House of Representatives, and judges in office on the effective date of this Constitution, and all other public officials who occupy positions corresponding to such positions as are recognized by this Constitution, shall not forfeit their positions automatically on account of the enforcement of this Constitution unless otherwise specified by law. When, however, successors are elected or appointed under the provisions of this Constitution, they shall forfeit their positions as a matter of course.

Date of Promulgation: November 3, 1946
Date of Enforcement: May 3, 1947.

APPENDIX I

BIBLIOGRAPHY

The mark (*) indicates a book especially useful for young readers, as well as for adults.

General

Borton, Hugh. *Japan's Modern Century.* New York: Ronald Press, 1970.
An excellent appraisal of the change from feudalism to industrialism.

Brzezinski, Zbignilw. *The Fragile Blossom: Crisis and Change in Japan.* New York: Harper & Row, 1972.
A scholarly account of Japan's growth.

Chaffee, Frederic H. et al. *Area Handbook for Japan.* Washington, D. C.: U. S. Government Printing Office, 1969.
A guidebook, including statistics and maps, to all aspects of Japan.

*DeBary, W. T. (ed.). *Sources of the Japanese Tradition.* New York: Columbia University Press, 1958.
A fine collection of primary works and introductory essays.

Duncan, William R. *Guide to Japan.* New York: International Publishing Service, 1971.
An illustrated survey.

*Keene, Donald, *Living Japan.* New York: Doubleday, 1959.
The story of Japan in superb photographs, with annotations.

*Reischauer, Edwin O. *The Story of a Nation.* New York: Knopf, 1970.
An illustrated, popular revision of an earlier work by the scholar and former ambassador.

Sansome, George. *A History of Japan.* 3 vols. Palo Alto: Stanford University Press, 1958–63.
A monumental work, showing the molding forces in Japanese society.

——— *Japan: A Short Cultural History.* New York: Appleton-Century, 1962.
The standard work in its field, from antiquity to the mid-nineteenth century.

*——— *The Western World and Japan.* New York: Knopf, 1950.
An excellent evaluation of the impact of the West on Japan.

Varley, H. Paul. *Japanese Culture: A Short History.* New York: Praeger, 1973.
A productive scholar's fresh account of national achievements.

*Webb, Herschel. *An Introduction to Japan.* New York: Columbia University Press, 1957.
A brief survey of Japan's history and culture.

Politics, Economics, and Government

Adams, T. F. & Hoshii, Iwao. *A Financial History of the New Japan.* Palo Alto: Kodansha, 1972.
An illustrated review of amazing growth.

Axelbank, Albert. *Black Star Over Japan: Rising Forces of Militarism.* New York: Hill and Wang, 1972.
Traces the roots of militarism and suggests they are not gone.

Dore, R. P. (ed.). *Aspects of Social Change in Modern Japan.* Princeton: Princeton University Press, 1967.
An incisive anthology concerning politics, sociology, and economics.

Hall, Robert B. *Japan: Industrial Power of Asia.* Princeton: Van Nostrand, 1963.
Traces the reasons for Japan's rapid industrial growth.

Kahn, Herman, *Emerging Japanese Superstate: Challenge & Response.* New York: Prentice-Hall, 1970.
The noted futurist's predictions for Japan's commercial impact.

Langer, Paul F. *Japan Yesterday and Today.* New York: Holt, Rinehart & Winston, 1966.
A volume in the Comtemporary Civilization Series.

McNelly, Theodore. *Politics and Government in Japan*. Boston: Houghton Mifflin, 1972.
    An illustrated, detailed study.

Maki, J. M. *Government and Politics in Japan: The Road to Democracy*. New York: F. A. Praeger, 1962.
    A good discussion of the transition from militarism to democracy.

Olson, Lawrence. *Japan in Postwar Asia*. New York: Praeger, 1970.
    An illustrated study of Japan's relationship to its neighbors.

Scalapino, Robert. *Democracy and the Party Movement in Prewar Japan*. Berkeley: University of California Press, 1953.
    A critical analysis of the formation of political parties and their attempts to introduce democratic government in the 1920's.

Religion and Philosophy

Anesaki, Masaharu. *History of Japanese Religion with Special Reference to the Social and Moral Life of the Nation*. Rutland: Tuttle, 1963.
    A rare analysis of the relationship between religion and society.

Bunce, W. *Religions in Japan*. Rutland: Tuttle, 1963.
    An excellent survey, with emphasis on Shinto, Buddhism, and Confucianism.

*DeBary, William Theodore, *The Buddhist Tradition in India, China and Japan*. New York: Random House, 1972. (Paperback).
    An excellent short collection of original documents.

Hearn, Lafcadio. *Japan's Religion: Shinto and Buddhism*. New Hyde Park: University Books, 1966.
    A classic study by a noted observer of Japan.

*Hori, I., et al. *Japanese Religion*. Palo Alto: Kodansha, 1972.
    An attractive pictorial.

Offner, C. *Modern Japanese Religions*. New York: Twayne Publishers, 1963.
    An evaluation of the changes in Japan's major religions.

Ono, Sokyo. *Shinto: The Kami Way*. Rutland: Tuttle, 1962.
    A popular introduction to Japan's indigenous religion.

Sociology and Customs

Asakawa, K. *The Early Institutional Life in Japan*. New York: Octagon, 1963.
    A unique work that examines traditional customs at their outset.

*Benedict, Ruth. *The Chrysanthemum and the Sword*. Boston: Houghton Mifflin, 1960.
    One of the best known sociological analyses about Japan.

Ishida, Takeshi. *Japanese Society*. New York: Random House, 1971.
    Traces the intricacies of relationships and conditions.

*Kato, H. *Japanese Popular Culture*. Rutland: Tuttle, 1962.
    A study of changing habits since World War II.

Suzuki, D. T. *Zen and Japanese Culture*. New York: Pantheon Books, 1959.
    An excellent study of Zen Buddhism and its impact on the arts of Japan.

*Vining, E. G. *Windows for the Crown Prince*. Philadelphia: Lippincott, 1952.
    A delightful story of the author's tutorship of the Japanese Crown Prince.

Vogel, Ezra F. *Japan's New Middle Class*. Berkeley: University of California Press, 1971.
    An Important contribution, analyzing a new force in Japan.

Literature and Art

*Akutagawa, R. *Rashomon and Other Stories*. New York: Liveright, 1952.
    A collection of fine Japanese fiction.

Bowers, Faubion. *Japanese Theatre*. New York: Hermitage House, 1952.
    An excellent survey of Japanese theatrical types, including the No, the Kabuki, and the Bungaku.

*Henderson, H. G. *An Introduction to Haiku*. New York: Doubleday, 1958.
    A study of Japan's most popular poetry, with translations and notes.

Hibbert, H. *The Floating World of Japanese Fiction*. New York: Oxford University Press, 1959.

178

An excellent study of writing during the early Tokugawa period (ca. 1680–1740), set against a background of the teahouses, shops, and theaters.

*KAWABATA, I. *Snow Country*. New York: Knopf, 1956.
A post-World-War-II novel, dealing with social conflict in Japan.

*KEENE, DONALD (ed.). *Anthology of Japanese Literature*. New York: Grove Press, 1955.
Excellent translations, ranging from the earliest times to the mid-nineteenth century.

*_____(ed.). *Modern Japanese Literature: An Anthology*. New York: Grove Press, 1957.
A supplement to Mr. Keene's earlier anthology.

*_____(ed.). *Twenty Plays of the No Theatre*. New York: Columbia University Press, 1970.
Recreates the splendor of an important part of Japan's culture.

*McCULLOUGH, H. (trans.). *The Taiheiki*. New York: Columbia University Press, 1959.
A literary classic of intrigue in the Japanese court during the fourteenth century.

*MORRIS, IVAN (ed.). *Modern Japanese Stories*. Rutland: Tuttle, 1962.
Fine translations of modern Japanese writing.

*_____ (ed. and trans.). *The Pillow Book of Sei Shonagon*. (2 vols.). New York: Columbia University Press, 1967.
An enduring work of scholarship, part of the "Records of Civilization, Sources & Studies Series."

*PAINE, R. AND SOPER, A. *The Art and Architecture of Japan*. Baltimore: Penguin Books, 1955.
An excellent introduction to techniques of Japanese art.

*SAIKAKU, I. *Five Women Who Loved Love*. Rutland: Tuttle, 1959.
One of the many delightful stories by the leading novelists of the era of the "Floating World."

*TANIZAKI, J. *Some Prefer Nettles*. New York: Knopf, 1955.
An outstanding novel of post-World-War-II Japan.

*TERRY, CHARLES S. *Masterworks of Japanese Art*. Rutland: Tuttle, 1956.
An excellent condensation of the six-volume work by the Tokyo National Museum.

*WALEY, ARTHUR (trans.). *The Tale of Genji*. London: Allen and Unwin, 1953.
A superb translation of Japan's greatest novel.

WARNER, LANGDON. *The Enduring Art of Japan*. New York: Grove Press, 1952.
A perceptive and comprehensive study.

179

APPENDIX J

INDEX

abortion, legalized, 102
Adams, Will, 51
agriculture, 5-7
Ainu, 3, 15
All-Japan Federation of Labor, 100
Amaterasu-O-mi-kami, 14, 15
American occupation, 97-102, 111
Amida Buddhism, 31, 35
Amur River Society, 79, 87
apprentice system, 111, 113
architecture, 26, 36, 42, 45, 118-19
area of Japan, 1
army, 68, 70, 84, 85, 88
art, 25, 26, 31, 36, 42, 58-59
Ashikaga Shogunate, 39-43
Asian Development Bank, 130
atomic bomb, 96, 125, 127
Australia, 81, 85
Axis Pact, 90, 91

bakufu, 34, 40
barley, 5-6
Basho, 59-60
Benedict, Ruth, 107
birth control, 2, 117
Bismarck, 69
British, 51, 64, 77, 80, 81, 88, 90, 91, 93, 95, 97
Buddha of Ultimate Reality. *See* Daimichi
Buddhism, 17, 18, 19, 22-25, 26, 29, 31, 35, 36, 38, 42, 43, 46, 74
bunraku, 60
Burma, 93, 94, 130
Burma Road, 90, 93
Bushido, 55

cabinet, 72, 76, 83-84, 85, 88
calligraphy, 31
capital, 19, 20, 27, 36, 51
Carolines, 79
Casablanca Conference, 95
castles, 45
centralization, 19, 32, 46, 53
Ch'an Buddhism. *See* Zen Buddhism.
charcoal, 7
Chiang Kai-shek, 86, 88, 90
Chikamatsu Monzaemon, 61
China, 13, 18, 19, 20, 29, 32, 36, 37-38, 43, 47, 51, 54, 62, 76-77, 80, 81, 83, 85, 86, 88, 89, 90, 91, 95, 96, 97, 104, 109, 121, 125, 127, 129

chonin class, 56, 57, 61
Choshu daimyo, 66
Chou En-lai, 127
Christianity, 48-50, 51, 52, 74
Churchill, Winston, 95
cities, development of, 55, 56, 62, 111, 117, 118-119
civil wars, 18, 39, 42
clans, 16, 18, 19. *See also* Minamoto; Satsuma; Soga; Taira
climate, 4
coal, 9
commended tenure, 33
Communist Party, 82, 98, 125
Communists, Chinese, 88, 100
Confucianism, 18, 21-22, 32, 54, 109, 110
conservation, 6, 7
constitution, 71-72, 87, 98, 99
constitution of articles, 17, 18
Coral Sea, Battle of, 94
Corregidor, Battle of, 93
cultured pearls, 8

Daimichi, 30
daimyo, 40, 44, 46, 48, 52-54, 56, 61, 64, 65, 66
dairy industry, 6
Darien, 78
Diet, 72, 76, 87, 98, 99, 121, 124, 125
Drifting Cloud, 75
dual economy, 123
Dutch, 52, 64, 91
Dutch East Indies, 91, 93, 94

East China Sea, 1
economy, postwar, 100, 101, 115-19, 126, 127
Edo, 51, 53, 56
education, 19, 73-75, 101, 112, 113, 123
Eisenhower, President, 125
elections, 98
electronics, 11-12, 116
emakimono, 36
emperor, 15, 19, 20, 25, 31, 32, 37, 39, 55, 64, 65, 71-72, 83, 88, 89, 96, 99, 101, 106, 110, 124
English (language), 119
Eta, 67, 110
Eugenic Protection Act, 102

Europeans. *See* British, Dutch, English, Christianity, Portuguese, Spaniards
extraterritoriality, 64, 76

family life, 16, 19, 75, 103–06, 108
feudalism, 32–34, 37, 44, 53–54, 56, 66, 67
firearms, 44
fire raids, U.S., 95
fish, 7
floating factories, 8
food, 2, 5, 115–16
foreign exchange, 8
forests, 5, 7
Formosa. *See* Taiwan
franchise, 83, 84, 98
Franciscans, 50
free tenure, 33
French, 80, 90
French Indochina, 90, 91
fruit industry, 6
fudai daimyo, 53
Fujiwara Clan, 18, 27, 29
Fujiwara Michinaga, 27
Futabatei Shimei, 75

Genro, 72
geography, 1
Germans, 79, 80, 81, 90, 96
Gilbert Islands, 93
Go-Daigo, Emperor, 38–39
gohei, 17
Golden Pavilion, 42
gomin-gumi, 61
government, 19, 22, 28, 31, 56, 66–72, 83, 97–102, 123–131
Greater East Asia Co-Prosperity Sphere, 90, 93
Guadalcanal, Battle of, 95
Guam, 93

haiku, 59–60
Hainan, 90
Hamaguchi Osachi, 86, 87
Hara, Prime Minister, 83
harbors, 3
harakari, 97
Harris, Townsend, 64
Hayotama Ichiro, 124
Heian Period, 27–31
Heian Shrine, 17
Hida Range, 3
Hideyoshi. *See* Toyotomi Hideyoshi
hierarchy, 68, 103–114
hiranga, 21, 30
Hirohito, Emperor, 96, 98, 101
Hiroshige, 59
Hiroshima, 96
Hitler, 90, 91
Hizen daimyo, 66

Hojo clan, 37, 43
Hojo Regency, 37, 39
Hokkaido, 2, 5, 6
Hokusai, 59
Honen Shonin, 35
Hong Kong, 93
Honshu, 2, 3, 15
Horyu-ji, 26
House of Councillors, 99
House of Peers, 72
House of Representatives, 72, 99
housing, 103, 104, 118–119, 122
Hull, Cordell, 92
hydroelectric power, 10

Ieyasu. *See* Tokugawa Ieyasu
Ikeda, Premier, 125
Imperial Rescript on Education, 74
Imperial Rule Assistance Association, 89
imports, 2, 7, 82, 115, 129
Indochina. *See* French Indochina
Indonesia, 130
industrialism, 43, 68–70, 117–18
industry, 9, 10, 69, 70, 99, 116, 117–18
Inland Sea, 3
Inukai, Prime Minister, 88
irrigation, 6
Ise, 43
islands (of Japan), 1, 2
isolation, policy of, 52
Issa, 60
Isshin, 64
Itagaki Taisuke, 70–71
Italians, 80, 90
Ito Hirobumi, 69, 70, 71, 79
Iwakura Mission, 69
Iwakura Tomomi, 69, 71
Izanami, 13
Izangi, 13
Izumo, 43

Japan Current. *See* Kuroshio
Japanese Alps, 3
Jesuits, 48
Jimmu-Tenno, 14
Jodo Buddhism, 35
jomon pottery, 13
judiciary, 99

kabuki, 42, 60
Kamakura, 31, 43
Kamakura Shogunate, 31–34, 36–37, 39
kami, 16
kamikaze, 38, 96, 106
kampaku, 27
kana, 21
kanji, 21
Kansai Plain, 2
Kanto Plain, 2, 29

Kato Komei, 79, 80, 84, 85
Kegon Buddhism, 24
kirisute gomen, 56
Kishi, Prime Minister, 124, 125
Kita Ikki, 87
Kiyomitsu, 59
Kiyonaga, 59
Komeito Party, 121
Konoye, Prince, 88-89, 92
Korea, 13, 17, 43, 46-47, 69, 78-79, 95, 130
Kublai Khan, 37, 38
Kuksai, 30
kumi, 19
Kurile Islands, 62, 96, 130
Kuroshio, 4
Kusha Buddhism, 24
Kwantung Army, 86, 87, 88, 89
Kyoto, 27, 28, 29, 31, 32, 39, 40, 43, 5
Kyoto Imperial University, 113
Kyushu, 2, 5, 13, 14, 15, 27, 38, 51

labor unions, 82, 83, 84, 100
lacquer, 26
land,
    geography, 2-3
    farms, 19
    See also soil
landowning, 18, 28, 33, 43, 70, 82, 100
language, 20, 30
Lansing-Ishii Agreement, 80
law, 18-19, 54-55, 74-75, 85, 99
League of Nations, 81, 85, 88
Liaotung Peninsula, 77, 86
Liberal Democratic Party, 120, 121, 129
Liberal Party, 70, 98, 124
literature, 20, 30-31, 59-60, 75
London Naval Conference, 87
Lotus Scripture, 35

Macao, 49
MacArthur, General Douglas, 97, 98, 100
magatama, 13
makimono, 31
Malaya, 13
Malayans, 13
Manchukuo, 88
Manchuria, 9, 78, 80, 86, 87, 88, 90, 96
Manchurian Incident, 87-88
Manchus, 88
Manila, 93
manpower, 10-11
Manyoshu, 21, 30
Mao Tse-tung, 127
Marco Polo Bridge, 89
Marianas Islands, 79, 95
Marshall Islands, 79
May 4th Movement, 81
Meiji Restoration, 65-66, 111
merchant class, 43, 56, 67
Midway, Battle of, 94

Midway Islands, 93, 94
migrations, 13-14
militarism, 32, 36, 39, 44, 65, 68-70, 73, 76, 79, 83-92, 94, 96, 99, 100
Minamoto Clan, 28-29, 37
Minamoto Yoritomo, 29, 31-32
minerals, 9
Ming Dynasty, 47
Missouri, USS, 96
Mitsubishi, 10-11
Mitsui, 10
mobility, social, 112-13
monasteries, 26, 36
money economy, 43, 56
Mongolia, 80
Mongols, 13, 37-38
monogatari, 30
Mononobe, 18
monopolies, 57
monsoon, 4
moral duty (*on*), 105, 106
most-favored nation, 66
Mount Fuji, 3
Mukden, 78, 88
Murasaki, Lady, 30
Muromachi, 40
Muso, 36
Mutsuhito, Emperor, 64-65
mythology, 13-15

Nagasaki, 49, 52, 96
Nagoya, 2, 47
Nakatomi, 17
Nanking, 89
Nara Period, 19-26
National Congress of Industrial Unions, 100
National Mobilization Law, 89
National Police Reserve, 124
navy, 84, 87, 94
Neo-Confucianism, 54
Neolithic Period, 13
Nichiren, 35, 43, 121
Nihongi, 21
Nippon, 15
Nobi Plain, 2
No drama, 41
nuclear testing, 124, 127, 129
nusa, 17

Oda Nobunaga, 44, 45, 49
Okinawa, Battle of, 95
Okinawa, possession of, 126
Okuma Shigenobu, 71
Olympic Games, 126
On. See moral duty
Opium War, 62
optical goods, 10
Oriental exclusion laws, U.S., 85

Osaka, 2, 11, 46, 48, 51, 56
Oyashio, 4, 5

paddy land, 6
painting, 36, 42, 58-59
parents, duty to, 104-109
parliamentary government, 70-73, 83, 89, 99-102
paternalism, 12
Peace Preservation laws, 85
Pearl Harbor, 92-93
peasants, 33-34, 57, 61-62, 67-68, 70, 86-87. *See also* feudalism
peerage, 66
Perry, Commodore, 63-64
Pescadore Islands, 77
petroleum, 9
Philippines, 78, 93, 130
Pillow Book of Sei Shonagon, 31
police, postwar, 101, 123, 124
politics, postwar, 120-127
polluting the self, 16
population, 2, 82, 102, 116-17
Port Arthur, 78
Portuguese, 44, 48, 49

Potsdam Declaration, 96
prehistory, 3, 13
press, 102, 132
priesthood, 17
primogeniture, 43
Progressive Party (Kaishinto), 71, 98, 124
Prussian influence, 69, 70, 71
Pure Land Buddhism, 35
purity, 16
Pu-yi, Henry, 88

railroads, 12, 70
rainfall, 4
regents, 18, 29, 48
reparations, 99, 130
rice, 5, 15
"rich country, strong arms," 66
ronin, 61
Roosevelt, F.D., 92, 96
Roosevelt, Theodore, 78, 79, 85
Roshana Buddhism, 25
rural life, 33, 82, 119-20
Russia, 8, 62, 64, 77-78, 88, 90, 121, 125, 130
Russian Revolution, 80
Russo-Japanese War, 77-78

Saigo Takamori, 69, 70
Saionji, Prince, 84
Sakhalin Island, 62, 78, 84, 96
samurai, 33, 40, 42, 44, 45, 52, 55, 56, 57, 60, 61, 65, 66, 67, 70, 72
San Filipe, 50
San Francisco, 85

sankin-kotai, 54
Sato, Prime Minister, 126
satori, 59-60
Satsuma, 64, 66, 69, 70
SCAP, 97, 98, 99, 100, 101
Sea of Japan, 1, 4
Sea of Okhotsk, 1, 4
seaweed, 9
seignors, 33, 34
Seii-Tai-shogun, 32
Seiyukai Party, 83
Sekigahara, Battle of, 48
Sengoku Jidai, 44
Shanghai, 89
Shantung Peninsula, 79, 80, 81, 86
shiki tenure, 33
shikken, 37
Shikoku, 2, 27
Shima Peninsula, 8
Shin Buddhists, 43
Shingon Buddhists, 29
Shinto, 16-17, 18, 24, 55, 74, 97, 108
Shinto shrines, 16
shipbuilding, 11, 52
shoens, 28, 33
shogun, 32, 40, 51, 53-54
Shotoku, Prince, 18
Siberia, 80, 84, 130
silk trade, 49, 86
silkworms, 82
Silver Pavilion, 42
Singapore, 93, 130
Sino-Japanese War, 76-77
snow, 9
Social Democrats, 98
Socialist Party, 82, 121, 124, 125
Soga Clan, 17-18
Sohyo, 121
soil, 6. *See also* land, geography
Solomon Islands, 93, 95
Sonno joi, 64
Southeast Asia, 91, 93, 94, 130
Soviet Union, 90, 91, 95, 96. *See also* Russia
Spaniards, 50
Stalin, Joseph, 95
strikes, postwar, 100
student protests, 122
suburbs, 118-19
Sumitomo, 10
sun worship, 15
Supreme Council of Japan, 96
Susa-no-wo, 14
Suzuki Kantaro, Admiral, 95

Taft-Katsura Agreement, 78
Taiho Codes, 19, 28
Taika Reforms, 18-19
Taira Clan, 28-29, 31

Taira Kiyomori, 29
Taiwan, 77
Tale of Genji, 30
Tanaka, General, 85, 86
Tanaka, Kakuei, 127, 129, 130-131
T'ang Dynasty, 1, 18, 19
tariffs, 129
taxes, 19, 27, 28, 33, 34, 56, 57, 62, 70
tea ceremony, 42
technology, 10-11, 49, 117-18
Tendai Buddhists, 29, 42, 43
Terauchi Masataki, 79
Thailand, 91
Tientsin, 90
Tojo Hideki, General, 88, 92, 93, 94, 95, 96
Tokaido Railway, 126
Tokugawa Hidetada, 51
Tokugawa Iemitsu, 51
Tokugawa Ieyasu, 44, 45, 48, 51, 52, 53
Tokugawa Peace, 62, 110
Tokugawa Shogunate, 51-64, 110
Tokyo, 2, 51, 95
Tokyo Imperial University, 73, 113
Tokyo-Yokohama earthquake, 82
tori-i, 16, 17
Toyotomi Hideyoshi, 44, 46-48, 51
tozama daimyo, 53, 62, 64
traditions in postwar life, 118
Treaty of Portsmouth, 78
Truman, President, 96
Tsushima, Strait of, 47
Tungus, 13
Twenty-One Demands, 79

ukiyo-e painting, 58-59
unconditional surrender, 95
United States, 62, 63, 78, 80, 85, 88, 89, 90, 91, 92, 93, 95, 96, 97, 99, 100, 115, 123, 126, 128, 129

universal manhood suffrage, 83, 84, 98
universal military conscription, 67
U.S.-Japanese Peace Treaty, 102
U.S.-Japanese Security Treaty, 125
Utamaro, 59

Versailles Conference, 80
Vietnam War, 128, 129
Vladivostok, 80

waka verse form, 30
Wake Island, 93
Washington Conference, 83-84
wheat, 5
Wilson, President, 80
women, 105
women's vote, 98
woodblock prints, 59
women, social position, 105
women's vote, 98
woodblock prints, 59
working conditions, 12
World Depression, 86-87
World War I, 79
World War II, 93ff

Xavier, Francis, 48-49

Yalta Conference, 95
Yamato Peninsula, 14, 15
Yamigata Aritomo, 68-69
Yasuda, 10
Yawata Company, 11, 130
Yayoi pottery, 13
Yokohama, 11, 31
Yoshida Shigeru, 98, 110, 123
Yuan Shih-kai, 80

zaibatsu, 10, 12, 70, 82, 86, 90, 100, 123
Zen Buddhism, 35-36, 42, 43, 50
Zengakuren, 122